High Flying

High Flying

by

Debra Allcock

First published 1999 by
The Industrial Society
Robert Hyde House
48 Bryanston Square
London W1H 7LN

© The Industrial Society 1999

ISBN 1 85835 592 3

Reprinted 1999, reference 986 tw9.99

The Industrial Society
Business Books Network
163 Central Avenue, Suite 2
Hopkins Professional Building
Dover
NH 03820
USA

**British Library Cataloguing-in-Publication Data.
A catalogue record for this book is available from the
British Library.**

Typeset by: Midlands Book Typesetting
Printed by: Cromwell Press
Cover by: Sign Design
Cover illustration by: Dave Cutler/SIS

The Industrial Society is a Registered Charity No. 290003

For Noreen Rimmer

Acknowledgements

The author would like to thank the following people for their invaluable advice, editorial comment, stories, ideas and support:

Keith Allcock for sharing his experiences

Louise Allcock for information on employment issues

Rachelle Peters for reading and suggesting improvements

Sheridan Maguire for his unerring crisp editorial comment

Andrew Forrest for reviewing and suggesting amendments

Dr Paul Farrand for his incisive comments on motivation

Helen Ripper for creating the time for the book to be written

Phil Newsam for her cutting financial acumen

Caroline Blaazar for her extensive knowledge of health and safety issues

Henry Scrope and Pat Bellamy for their advice on employment law

Dr John Edmondson for his analogies and simple explanations

Contents

Introduction

When I was promoted to my first management role I was naturally really pleased. I had always believed from watching my own line manager that I could do the job better, and indeed better than our head of department. Frankly, I was never really sure what they did with their days anyway. Looked pretty easy to me.

Well, it didn't turn out to be quite a simple as I had thought! To be honest, in the beginning, my behaviour was not dissimilar to one of those line managers the cartoonist Scott Adams describes in his Dilbert series. I didn't handle the 'power' that goes with being a manager at all well and mistook being bossy for managing.

I was promoted to be manager from within the team that I was already working in. Many of the team members were my friends. I didn't know how to make the transition from being a team-mate to a colleague and behaved not unlike Genghis Khan! Unsurprisingly, they began to really dislike me. Of course, I had been told that I didn't need to be liked, only respected. Well, I think it's fair to say they didn't respect me much either.

I did some ridiculous things. The team I managed were responsible for setting up and running courses for international delegates, for booking speakers, organizing the venues, taking the bookings, etc. Each member was responsible for a certain part of the world.

I remembered reading somewhere that you were supposed to set targets for your team. I wasn't quite sure why, but it sounded like a good thing to do, so off I went enthusiastically setting targets. However, I didn't really think through why targets should be set. So I set all sorts of extremely odd and usually completely irrelevant targets. One I remember vividly was for the administrator for Europe to write a paper on the role of trade unions in Europe and their impact on the UK!

It all culminated in a team meeting about three months into the job. I had a go at the team for their performance and they retaliated by making it very clear to me how poorly I was performing in my new job.

It made me think. I suddenly realized that I had been badly at fault. That these people were in fact a team of individuals who really wanted to do a good job themselves and see me do a good job, and that instead of helping them I was hampering them.

I admitted I had been getting it wrong, told them that I wanted to get it right and that I needed them to help me and then, most importantly, I really listened to what they had to say. It worked. Things improved and so did I. Even today, many years later, I can truly say that one of the happiest times in my working life was that very first management job.

I am telling you this because, if I had had some training or been able to read a book like this before I started the job, I might not have made these mistakes. Hopefully, by reading this book you will not fall into some of the more obvious traps that await a person who is being a manager for the very first time.

'If a man's foresight were as good as his hindsight, we would all get somewhere.' [American Proverb]

CHAPTER 1

What do managers do?

'Choose a job you love and you'll never have to work a day in your life.' [Confucius]

When you become a manager for the very first time, you are no longer judged on the quality of work you produce, but on the quality of work your team produces. You become accountable for both your own work and that of the people in your team. And that takes some getting used to.

Probably, like me, you began your career specializing in a technical area. Some of you may have followed a path to promotion that looks something like this:

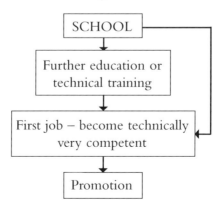

This is called the promotion funnel and looks like this:

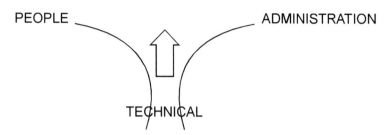

PEOPLE   ADMINISTRATION

TECHNICAL

Most of us get promoted because we are very good at our current technical job. This can be anything from typing to accountancy, from bricklaying to architecture.

Someone notices how good you are technically (and sees other qualities as well), and you are given promotion. Or you apply for a new job and are promoted on the basis of your past performance.

Suddenly you find yourself on a higher salary, with more responsibility. Your job fundamentally changes. It goes from being mainly technical to including administration (which is the lot of every manager), budgets, personnel administration, monthly reports, etc.

The administrative side is fairly easy to pick up, and there is usually someone to show you what to do and guidelines about what needs to be done, how it needs to be done and by whom and when.

The key difference between your new job as a manager and your old job is that you become responsible for other people. You are accountable for their motivation, performance and timekeeping.

People are not as easily dealt with as the end-of-month figures or the monthly report. They can be unpredictable, emotional, erratic, irrational, challenging and you may find that dealing with them is the hardest part of the manager's job.

And if any manager tells you that he or she doesn't find people challenging to work with then I'll show you a manager who doesn't really understand people.

The thing about people is that you can say exactly the same thing to two of them and get an entirely different reaction. You can say something to the *same person* on one day and on the next and get a different reaction! You can't predict how they are going to think about things or react to circumstances or information. Even when they normally behave very predictably, one day they surprise you. Although I have to say that, almost without exception, the surprises that I have experienced from the people I have managed have been good ones. People so often amaze with their creativity, humanity, humour and sheer willingness to get on and do the best job that they can.

You can curse a computer that doesn't do what you need it to do. If you curse at a person they either curse back or harbour a grudge. What sometimes happens, because people can be so difficult to deal with, is that new leaders will slip back down the promotion funnel into the technical side of the job, because it's easier there and they know what they're doing.

It's rarely because they're lazy. More often it's because no one has ever taught them how to lead and manage people.

Being a manager is the most challenging job I have ever had — and it is also the most rewarding.

So, the main difference between being a manager and being a technician is the fact that as a technician you are responsible solely for your own work — its timeliness, delivery, quality, etc. As a manager you are responsible for the work, timeliness, delivery and quality of your team. You are also responsible for their motivation and their ability to work well together as a team.

Levels of manager

No matter how big or small your organization, in the UK there are essentially five levels of management.

- Chair of the Board and Board Members
  Usually non-executive, i.e., they are not employed full-time by the company, they advise and monitor the performance of the Chief Executive and directors
- Chief Executive/General Secretary/Director General
  Accountable for the running of the whole organization
- Directors/Senior managers
  Work with the Chief Executive and senior management team to achieve the organization's strategic objectives and are often accountable for a division of the organization

- Middle managers/Heads of department
  Usually accountable for a department, its team members and the achievement of departmental objectives
- First line managers/Supervisors/Team leaders
  Usually accountable for a smaller team within a department or division.

Organizational structures

Most UK organizations have a non-executive board (in the case of charitable organizations this would normally be trustees) to whom the Chief Executive reports. The board is normally appointed by the shareholders of a company to look after their interests in the running of the company. Or, in the case of a charitable organization, board members are appointed by fellow trustees. The board is accountable for determining the strategic direction of the organization, its financial viability and progress towards achieving its objectives.

Most boards have a high degree of legal accountability to shareholders for the performance of the organization although some members do not have an executive role. Many board members are running other businesses or sitting on the boards of more than one organization.

The Chief Executive is normally appointed by, and reports to, the board.

The Chief Executive

The Chief Executive Officer (CEO) of an organization (or Secretary General or Director General) is the person who is accountable for implementing the strategic direction of the organization and the day-to-day running of it. He or she is also accountable for the overall management of all the staff and for providing vision and direction as well as achieving the organization's financial objectives.

CEOs are often very remote from the detailed running of the organization and spend the bulk of their time managing people and thinking ahead. They get most of their information from their directors.

Directors/Senior managers

These people work closely with the CEO to achieve the organization's objectives and set new ones for the future. They are usually fairly remote from the shop floor or front line operations of the organization.

They will normally be heavily dependent on the information given to them in direct reports from middle management. They will probably feel they have a certain degree of freedom in how to achieve the objectives the organization has set and will feel a high degree of ownership for those goals as they will have been involved in setting them.

Most first line managers won't come across them during the normal course of their work.

Middle managers/Heads of departments

Middle managers and heads of departments are sometimes in a very vulnerable position. Nowadays, mass reductions in staff are common and middle managers are often the first to go. They can feel caught between you (the first line manager) and your team and the more senior managers within the organization. They will spend much of their time managing their departments and trying to achieve local objectives that fit into the wider whole. They will often not have all the information they need to carry out their duties. They have a particularly difficult job, because unlike you they do not have direct control over the actions and performance of the front line staff and have to do it all through their first line managers and team leaders, i.e., you! Plus, they will be the ones who have to handle the 'flak' from the senior managers in the organization.

This is a uniquely stressful position, for many reasons. They have to trust and rely on people, like you, who are very often inexperienced in a management role and yet have massive influence on the organization's performance as a whole because they are the ones managing the 'workers'. Alternatively, they have to rely on people who are very experienced and have a massive impact on how easily (or not as the case may be) the head of department can carry out their job.

Spare a thought for the tough life of a middle manager/head of department. One day it could be you!

First line manager/Team leader

This is you

You will be accountable for a team with a very specific remit and clear accountabilities. Most of your duties will be day-to-day operational ones. Your job is crucial to the organization and you are very important because everything that higher management needs to achieve is through you. Only through you can they reach the people who actually operate the machinery, provide the service, speak to the customer, look after the patient, mix the cement, care for the child, type the report, process the accounts...

How did I get here?

You will probably have reached your position as first line manager through one of three routes.

1 You were externally promoted and are completely new to both the organization and the team.
2 You were internally appointed but from a different team within the organization.
3 You were promoted from within the team you are now managing.

All of these routes have their pros and cons.

External appointment

Pros	Cons
● They don't know you ● They don't have any negative expectations of you based on previous experience or gossip ● You can bring fresh ideas to the running of the team ● You have the opportunity to get to know them without the influence of other people's opinions ● They are more likely to accept new ideas from you because you are not held back by past experience	● They don't know you ● They don't have any positive expectations of you based on previous experience or knowledge ● You have no history with the team and therefore may not understand why they do things as they do ● You only see how they are with you, you don't have the opinions or experience of others to guide you ● They may view your new ideas with suspicion because you don't 'understand' the organization or its culture

Internal appointment

Pros	Cons
● You have a good understanding of the organization already, in particular its culture ● The team will already know of you by repute and may already be prepared to respect you ● People may be more willing to listen to your ideas because they believe you know the organization ● You will have some good networks from within the organization, particularly your old team	● You may have some preconceived ideas and opinions and be over-influenced by the existing culture ● The team already know of you by reputation and may be suspicious of you ● There may be a member of the team who applied for the job and didn't get it who feels some resentment ● Adversaries within the organization whom you already had will still be there

Appointed from within the team

Pros	Cons
● You already know everyone ● You have a good understanding of the work of the team and will have experienced at first hand what doesn't work ● You will know what worked and didn't work well with the previous manager ● You will have access to internal networks within the organization and the team ● You get the chance to lead your team and see them grow and develop	● You already know everyone ● You will be so close to how the team has worked in the past that it may be difficult to be objective ● You may be trying to be different to or the same as the previous manager ● You will have to tap into existing networks which can be hard for a newcomer ● You will have to stand back from the team and may have to make hard decisions about your personal friends ● You will have to make the difficult transition from team member to team manager and *it is very different*

The main difference between being an employee and being the manager

The main difference you will notice is that you are now expected to support the management line even when you don't agree with it. Your loyalty will need to be primarily to the organization and not to the team. This is difficult, especially because you are still working so closely with your team.

You will no longer be able to join in the group whinges about the organization or the management (because after all you are now one of them and must not be disloyal or critical about your colleagues, just as you wouldn't want them to criticize you to their teams).

Finally, you become accountable for the performance of each and every individual within your team. If they are not performing you will be held to account and expected either to get them to perform or get them to leave. Either way, you can no longer tolerate complacently the weaker members of the team sure in the knowledge of your own ability. From now on, the performance of the team will be the measure of your performance and effectiveness as the manager. You will be measured not on how you perform the technical side of the job, but on how well you manage the processes and lead the people within your team to achieve the overall objective of the team.

Scared? Regretting it already? Feeling overwhelmed?

I can assure you that through good times and bad, ups and downs, working with a group of people on a common goal, achieving success and seeing them grow as a result of your efforts is incredibly rewarding.

'Success is a science; if you have the conditions right you'll get the result.'
[Oscar Wilde (1883)]

Summary and key points

- You are now on the first rung of the management ladder.
- You are the manager with key power to deliver the organization's objectives.
- Whichever route you got the job, there are pros and cons.
- It is a wonderful job!

CHAPTER 2

Starting your new job as manager

'"Where shall I begin, please your majesty?", he asked. "Begin at the beginning," the King said gravely, "and go on until you come to the end; then stop."' [Lewis Carroll, *Alice in Wonderland* (1865)]

It's the first day of your new job as a manager. You will either be walking into a completely strange organization, or a familiar organization but a different team, or the same team but simply to a different desk.

Whichever, you will probably be feeling very nervous (although hopefully excited as well) and wondering what to do and how to make clear the fact that you are now a manager without trampling all over people.

The thoughts running through your head probably go something like this:

'I'm not sure that I'm doing the right thing'
'They'll never take me seriously'
'What should I say first?'
'Will they be friendly to me?'
'Will I be able to cope with the work?'
'What will I do if I make a mistake?'
'How will I establish my credibility as a manager?'

and so on.

They are the same thoughts that, at every level, everybody in an organization has at some point when starting a new job. They are completely normal and are simply a sign that you care and want to do a good job. So, how do you prepare yourself so that your first few days on the job are as effective as you want them to be?

Induction plans

Ask for an induction plan which lays out exactly what you need to learn, from whom and in what order. You should have such a plan even if you have been promoted from within the team. The kinds of things that you should ask to be included in an induction plan are:

- Your terms and conditions of employment (which are highly likely to have changed now you have stepped on to the management ladder).
- Information and an introduction to the workings of the organization and the team.
- Disciplinary and grievance procedures (these are particularly important because whereas before you might have used them or been subject to them, now you will actually have to implement them).
- Fire and bomb procedures – your team's welfare and safety is now a priority for you.
- Other codes and guidelines such as standards of dress, smoking policies, etc.
- Your responsibilities for health and safety (more on this in Chapter 9).
- What training you need to attend in what period – this should either be arranged for you in advance or you should be told how to arrange it.
- What people you need to meet (it's often a good idea actually to arrange the meetings with them yourself).
- What administrative duties you will be expected to carry out, to what standards and timescales.
- A series of one-to-one meetings with your new team members so that you can get to know them individually.

● A one-to-one with your line manager once a week for at least the first month followed by one-to-ones at least once every month.

So, what are the best ways to begin your time as a manager?

Day one

Take it easy on day one. Spend the time getting to understand the bare basics such as how the telephone is answered and where things are generally kept as well as completing all the administrative forms that tend to come with a new appointment. Spend some of the day chatting with your new team and getting to know them (I would suggest informally), although try not to be too disruptive of their jobs. Ask your own line manager to give you some time on the first day, towards the end of the day, so that you can chat about what has come up and ask any questions that have become obvious.

In addition this is an opportunity for you to clarify with your own line manager the limits of your authority, exactly what he or she expects of you, and for you to begin building your relationship with them. It is as important to have a good relationship with your own boss as it is for you to have a good one with your team. You need your boss's support.

Make it clear to the team that you are aware that you are new to the job and that you are willing to learn from them. This includes those of you promoted from within. You may well know how the team works and how to do your old job inside out, but the manager's job is completely new to you and will be different. Your team will not normally expect you to be perfect at it from day one.

Be prepared to ask stupid questions if you need to. Any question to which you don't know the answer is not a stupid one. The stupid thing is not to ask and then make a big mistake later!

By the end of week one

You will make it to the end of the first week. You probably faced a problem of some kind during this first week and dealt with it.

If you did, congratulations. If you haven't faced one yet you will soon. Don't panic however; Marcus Aurelius said *'Do not fear the problems of the future. You will meet them armed with the same weapons of reason and logic that arm you against today'*.

By the end of this week, you should have met most of the key people in the organization that you will have to work with on a regular basis. This will almost undoubtedly have included the accounts department, the personnel department and any others that you and your new team are likely to be dealing with.

You should also have a fairly good idea of what is expected of you in the job. Try to make sure that you have another one-to-one with your boss during the first week so that you can go through what you've learned during the week and any other questions that have cropped up.

It's a good idea to take your new team out to lunch in the first week if the organization is prepared to pay for it. Otherwise, simply ask everyone to join you in the pub, or wherever else is suitable. This is a good way to get to know the team informally, and you are likely to find out things that would not normally be said in the office.

Learning about your team

The best way to really learn about your team is to listen to them. However, some initial background research will be useful. You should have copies of their personnel files. Look through to establish their histories and their experience. This is also a really good way of discovering if any of them have hobbies which hide talents you could use, such as being treasurer of the local sports club (they could maybe help you look after the monthly accounts).

However, most of what you find out about your team will be because you spend time getting to know about their jobs and what they actually do, before straying into the more personal areas of their home lives and hobbies.

You should have a one-to-one with each member of your team within the first two weeks of the job so that you can get to know them and they can get to know you. I will talk in more detail about how to handle one-to-ones later. Do, however, make sure that during the one-to-one you ask them what they enjoy most about their jobs, what they enjoy least and the one change they would like to see you make to either the team or their jobs. Don't make any promises that you're not sure you can keep, but do listen carefully and objectively. Make notes throughout the one-to-one so that they can see you are listening and that you are so interested in what they have to say you're writing it down. Quite apart from anything else, it will help you to remember.

I'll talk more about how else to use a one-to-one in Chapter 7. However, I would recommend in this first one-to-one that you ask each of them what they look for in a leader and what it is that you could do to support them most in their jobs. As they probably haven't been asked this before, first it will help them to see that you really care and want to do a good job, and secondly, it will tell you what sort of leadership they are looking for.

The other thing to do to make sure you are constantly learning about your team is to walk the job. This means going to their desk or place of work to chat with them. Don't make the mistake of thinking that just because your desks are a few feet apart that you know what's going on or that you don't need to walk the job. People find it a lot easier to say what's on their mind if you are on their territory where they feel comfortable, safe and at home.

Above all, find out about the jobs that they do. Not because you have to do them but so that you really understand what they enjoy, what the difficulties are, how their relationships work within the team and across functions within the organization.

Where to sit

When I was 'growing up' in the working world, managers always had either an office to themselves or the best desk by the window. Somehow it seemed to go with the job – that the manager got the perk of the most comfortable desk, chair, most up-to-date equipment and the best spot in the room. I never questioned it really, it seemed something to aspire to, although I suppose deep in the recesses of my mind it felt a little unfair.

The world has changed, thank goodness. Good managers now look to their team's comfort first. You, the manager, need to put the welfare and comfort of your team first. You should have the worst position in the room, the oldest furniture, the most uncomfortable chair, if need be, although clearly, ideally, you and all your team would have the best equipment and furniture to do the job.

You do need to sit where you can see and be seen, but try to avoid sitting where it is apparent that you are the boss. Your status as a leader should be dependent upon your behaviour, not upon external trappings. It's not the desk that makes the manager but the lack of one. Actually, I sometimes think managers ought not to be allowed to have desks of their own at all, it only encourages them to sit at them when they really should be walking around, talking to their teams and working alongside them.

Showing you're the leader

Establishing yourself as the leader takes time. You need time for your team to realize that they can trust you and for you to demonstrate that you trust them. Despite what may seem common sense, you are more likely to demonstrate your leadership by asking others what decisions they think ought to be made than just leaping in and making them yourself because it appears to be your job. Demonstrating leadership is a crucial part of the job – see Chapter 3 for more advice.

Getting some training

Whatever else you ask for in your first few days as a manager you *must* ask for some training in how to be a leader and how to manage a team. Whilst this book is of course a start, it can never be as good as an event where you sit down with others in the same boat as you and share experiences and real-life issues. In a book I can only make some generalizations which may or may not be applicable to your situation. On a course you will have the opportunity to talk about the *real* issues that face you.

Catching a coach

It is also a good idea in your first management position to find yourself a coach or mentor, either within the organization or from outside.

A coach can help you to recognize what kinds of things you can do differently in order to be more effective as a manager and can help you to work out the solutions to particular problems.

A mentor is someone within the organization who is normally not directly involved in your work, or the work of your team, but who can give you advice and support you, not just in this job, but in your career in the organization.

The advantage of having someone from within the organization is that they know the internal politics and the people involved. The advantage of having someone from outside the organization is that they have no particular axe to grind and are more able to be objective and focus on you. You can share ideas, phone up if you're unsure about how to tackle a particular problem, describe how you have dealt with things and get their feedback on how they think you're doing.

Summary and key actions

- Make sure you have a well planned induction.
- Take time to learn about your team.
- Sit where you can see and be seen.
- Ask for training in leadership and management.
- Have regular meetings with your own line manager.

CHAPTER 3

Your role as leader

Now you are the manager one of the very first things that you need to do is to learn the difference between management and leadership. There are of course some historic misconceptions about management and leadership. There is a very clear and distinct difference between the two elements of the job that you have taken on and it is important that you recognize these early.

Management is essentially the term that describes the actions that an individual takes around 'things'. That is, processes, structures, plans, resources, equipment, money, machinery, and so on.

Leadership is the term that describes the actions that an individual takes around people.

There are many different definitions of the distinction between leadership and management. One of my own particular favourites is that accredited to Sir John Harvey-Jones, ex-Chairman of ICI and latterly famed for his role in the *Troubleshooter* series filmed for the BBC where he advised organizations on how to improve their results. He said 'Leadership is the art of getting extraordinary results out of ordinary people'. Peter Drucker, another management guru, is famously quoted as saying 'So much of what we call management consists of making it hard for people to work'.

So, essentially, you manage processes and lead people. But why is it important to make the distinction? And why do you need to know about it? Well, because it is how effective you are in your role as a leader that is going to have the biggest impact on the success of your team and ultimately, therefore, the success of your organization. Poor leadership accounts for more of the troubles faced by organizations than almost any other single cause. And poor leadership, as we all know, affects not only the organization but the economy and country as a whole. Good leaders are vital and you are now one of the people we will all be expecting to lead us to success.

It is important that you are aware of how the emphasis on the term leadership has changed. These days, it is not enough to know *how* to be an effective leader. You also need to understand *why* leadership matters.

Among the many reasons why leadership matters, there are just three I am going to mention here: the changing world of work, the impact of technology and the economic imperative.

The changing world of work

The world of work has changed dramatically and is continuing to do so. For example, the pattern of employment in the UK has undergone significant alterations.

Statistics show that there has been a 70% increase in the numbers of self employed who now make up 3.4 million people. You probably know someone yourself who is self-employed or who sub-contracts to someone who runs their own business. All of these self-employed people will need to be effective leaders in their own businesses to achieve success.

People in the workforce are also less likely simply to stay with their current employer out of loyalty. One out of six UK employees stays with their employer less than one year. One out of two stay less than five years. What will make the difference to whether they stay or go? It may be how well they are led.

Organizations themselves are finding it harder to survive long term. They either go out of business or get swallowed up by larger corporations. Again, you could argue that effective leadership is what is going to make the difference to organizational survival.

Then there is the change to structure in organizations. You yourself have probably been subjected to such changes in working practices as loss of jobs or restructuring of accountabilities. Many organizations have been introducing flatter structures, encouraging their managers to delegate decision taking further down the line, introducing the concept of empowerment and so on. This clearly means that leaders need to be stronger, more effective and more enabled.

There has a been a resulting loss of job security for many people, which might explain why they are less likely to remain with one employer for a considerable length of time. Employers now are forced to look at creating employability because they can no longer be relied upon to create employment. And to look at how they can attract and retain the best people. But more importantly, how to get the most out of the people they have got, for as much of the time as they have them. And it's leadership that will make the biggest impact here. *Your* leadership.

The impact of technology

It hardly seems worth mentioning technology here. Not because it isn't important but because not one of us is able in any way to avoid its impact. It has become so much a daily part of our lives that I suspect most of us are unaware of it. For example, did you know that today's consumer wears more computing power on their wrist than existed in the whole world before 1961? That there is more computer power in a Sega game than it took to put a man on the moon?

Just look at the impact the mass globalization of technology has had on communication, for example the internet. A friend of mine, Chris Bourne, has a son, Joe, who has gone to be a doctor in Sierra Leone. Chris and his wife were somewhat concerned about how they would keep in contact with him. Chris was stunned to receive an e-mail from Joe, who said that there he was in the middle of Sierra Leone, the only doctor serving 30,000 people, and with no running water, sending an e-mail on a laptop, powered by a battery because there is no mains electricity, via satellite to his father thousands of miles away. Amazing! No water – but he had access to technology.

With technology meaning faster information, faster responses and the demand that creates, it will be leaders who have a major role to play, not just in ensuring that their teams and their organizations keep up, but that the individuals with whom they work are feeling fulfilled and contributing to work.

The economic imperative

There is also an economic imperative for having well trained, effective leaders. First, poor leadership costs money, wastes resources, wastes people. It has been said that one of the chief concerns of today's business executives is the large number of unemployed on the payroll! People who are not contributing as much as they would like or are being allowed to. We need successful organizations, whether they are profit-making or charitable, local government or otherwise. For example, there is about to be a massive change in the age profile in the UK. In the next 20 years, more than half of the population will be older than the people working. Organizations need to be successful so that they can survive. Because we will need healthy organizations to help to support an ageing population.

There is also the cost of absenteeism. A survey conducted by The Industrial Society in 1997 said that the average number of days per year people in the UK were absent is 8.26. Let's say that there are approximately 22 million people at work and that these people are taking an average of 8.26 days. That is a massive annual loss to UK business. The thing that particularly galls me is that as I only had two days off last year – somebody has had my share!

The question is 'Are these days genuine?'. Maybe, and maybe some stem from what we could call motivation sickness. You know, you may have experienced them yourself. Those days when you have a slight headache, nothing major, but you wake up feeling slightly off colour and cannot face going into work. This is perhaps because the work is boring or stressful or you are not enjoying it. Or you don't feel valued or appreciated.

Now just imagine that you could get the people who feel like that on those cold Mondays to work for only one extra day and thereby reduce the average number of days absent to 7.26 days. You would add 22.7 million days to work.

A recent survey on absenteeism in the UK's National Health Service showed that there was less absenteeism in Trusts where communication between workers and management was emphasized, where there was more staff training available and greater control and flexibility for staff in their jobs. Precisely the sort of thing that we need leaders to make happen. An Industrial Society survey of attitudes to work showed that 33% of people surveyed said they could do more. Remember, there is no traffic jam on the extra mile.

You, the leader, are what could make the difference between people coming to work or staying at home.

So what?

Hopefully you will now have a good understanding of why leadership is the most important part of your job. Ralph Waldo Emerson said: 'The man who knows how will always have a job, the man who knows why will always be his boss.'

But what does it mean for you? Well, one of my favourite stories is this one which I feel beautifully illustrates the difference between management and leadership.

Management and leadership

A British company and a Japanese company decided to hold a competitive staff boat race on the River Thames. The Japanese won the first race by a mile. The British became discouraged and morale at the company sagged. Senior managers decided the reason for this defeat had to be found. So an internal project team was set up to investigate the cause and recommend appropriate action. This report identified that the Japanese team had eight people rowing and one person steering. The British company, in contrast, had one person rowing and eight people steering. Senior management at the British company hired a consultant to study the British team's structure. Several months later they concluded in a leather-bound report that too many people were steering and not enough were rowing.

An action plan was immediately put into place to prevent the Japanese from winning again. The British

> team structure was changed to four Rowing Managers, three Senior Rowing Managers, an Executive Rowing Manager and a Rower. A performance and appraisal system was set up to give the person rowing the boat more incentive to work harder and become a key performer.
>
> The next race was won by the Japanese by an increased margin of two miles. The British company reacted by laying off the rower due to his poor equipment and halting development work on a new boat. They gave a high performance award to the consultant and distributed the rest of the money made to senior management.

Action-centred Leadership – the 'doing' part of leadership

There are essentially two parts to leadership – the 'doing' part and the 'being' part. The doing part is the easier bit and so I will cover it first.

Some years ago, John Adair developed a model of leadership based on research into what makes an effective leader. He called this model 'action-centred leadership' and it is essentially a functional model. In other words, it is primarily based on what leaders do rather than who they are or what they know.

In simple terms an action-centred leader focuses on the actions that can be taken in three main areas – the achievement of the task, building and maintaining a team and developing individuals within the team. This can be represented by a simple model (see opposite).

As the model demonstrates, you need to be effective in all three areas in order to be effective overall. Although it might seem that the place to concentrate your efforts is in the 'achieve the task' circle, further thought will show you that this is clearly not the case. First, any action you take in one circle impacts on the other.

I'm sure you can think of a manager you have experienced yourself in the past who was very task focused. And I expect you found that this manager took little notice of individuals, other than those who also focused on the task, and had no interest in team building. And of course, the consequence of this is that the

**Action–centred
Leadership model**

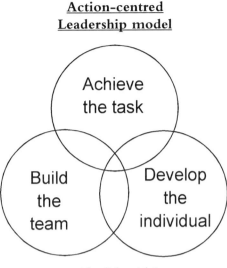

After John Adair

individuals get fed up, the team fall out and the job doesn't get done because the leader needs both the team and the individual in order to achieve the task.

And a leader who focuses on the team circle at the expense of the task will find that it is very difficult to achieve good team work without a task to focus on. And that having a task on which to concentrate is one of the easiest ways to create a team spirit.

Finally, a leader who focuses on individuals, and has favourites, has little or no hope of achieving the overall task or engaging the team in co-operating with each other.

Don't make the mistake of thinking that you will never exhibit favouritism or have favourites. It's almost impossible not to.

Human beings, by their very nature, like some people more than others. And it is very difficult not to show it, despite your best efforts. There really will be some people in your team who are exceptional workers, have a positive attitude and are always willing to help. And there will be others who are less reliable, a bit whingey and critical and who may not like you. It is hard to retain impartiality about these two different kinds of people.

You see, favouritism at work doesn't exhibit itself in favours given or special things done. It generally manifests itself in who gets the 'best' jobs to do. And you will, of course, argue logically for giving the best and most important jobs to the most reliable and talented worker, because you need the job done well. But your team probably won't see it like that. They are highly unlikely to think they are less capable than the other person. So, in addition to the difficulties within the team created by favouritism you will find you become dependent upon one or two key people. Then what happens when they are sick, or if they leave? It's not just about being seen to be fair. It makes sense to develop *everyone* in your team. It makes sense to let everyone have some responsible jobs and some boring ones. Otherwise you'll only create problems for yourself in terms of your ability to deliver the team's objectives and get the task done.

So, to recap, in order to be an effective leader you need to ensure that you take actions to achieve the task, to build the team and to develop the individuals.

There are five stages of leadership – which can be translated into a simple framework – which makes a useful toolbox for you to use when evaluating your effectiveness as a leader.

Define objectives

You need to be really clear what it is that you are trying to achieve as a team. It is important here not to confuse what your team does with what its objective is. The job may be to process invoices, the objective may be to ensure that the organization has a healthy cash balance at the end of each month.

As the leader you need to think in terms of objectives and allow the team to concentrate on how to achieve them. To do this, you need to be clear about the purpose of your own job, the purpose of the team and how these both fit into the overall aims and objectives of the organization.

Plan

This is the stage at which you need to make sure that you have as much of the information and resources available as you are likely to need in order to achieve the task. Planning is of course an ongoing process and you will need to spend a lot of time consulting with people – both within your team and in other parts of the organization – because they will have more of the information and resources you need than you will.

It is important to consult with people before making a decision. Not just because it is the right thing to do, but because, first, through consultation, you find out information that may crucially affect your outcomes and, second, because when people feel they have been genuinely consulted, they are much more likely to support whatever decision you take, even if it is not the decision they want.

Brief

You obviously need to tell people that you have made a decision, what that decision is and how it needs to be implemented. You may already have a formal briefing system in your organization and I will explain more about its importance and your role in it in Chapter 7.

Monitor and support

A key part of your role is to monitor what is going on in your team and provide support where necessary. Please note I have deliberately avoided the use of the word 'check'. I dislike the word myself because it implies a lack of trust and a level of status which I don't think is helpful to the modern manager/leader.

Anybody doing a job for the first time is bound to make mistakes. Actually, mistakes are rather a good thing because they help people to learn and they show us new ways of doing things, even if it is by accident. Penicillin was discovered as the result of a mistake, and so were post-it notes.

The diagram overleaf explains very simply how to monitor and provide support appropriately; that is, in a way that the person being monitored does not feel checked on, but supported. Always remember to tell people that you will be monitoring progress. You don't have to be formal about it or make it sound like checking. Saying something simple like, 'I'll pop in tomorrow morning to see how you're getting on with that project and if you need any help', or 'Let me know at the end of the week where you've got to so I can see how we're doing' is perfectly OK.

Most people, when doing a job for the first time, or in fact

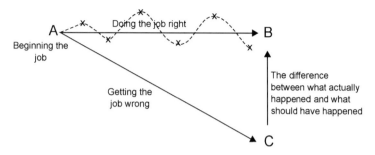

x: The point at which you monitor

doing any job, rarely manage to go from A to B in a perfectly straight line without making the odd mistake along the way. The key thing is not that they made a mistake, but that because you are monitoring and supporting them, you pick up the mistake when it is only minor and can be easily corrected. Not monitoring means a mistake might get missed and then the person won't get the job right and you will be forced to tell them that they failed. A little early monitoring will avoid that.

Incidentally, be careful when pointing out mistakes. It is very easy just to point out what isn't right. You need always to be looking for what is right as well so that you can point out what's going well at the same time. However, make it real, otherwise people will stop believing you when you praise them.

Never be tempted to fix people's mistakes for them. Always talk through what went wrong and what could be done to put it right.

Evaluate

Finally, of course, you need to evaluate the progress of the task, both during it and at the end. The odd thing about evaluation is that we tend to talk a lot about the things that went wrong and what we should do better next time, and very little about the things that went well that we could repeat. Remember to evaluate the things done well and make sure you point out those that could be repeated.

Framework for leadership

This very simple framework (below) pulls together all the things you need to remember to do as an action-centred leader. In an ideal world you would start at the beginning of a task and work through the framework to the end. However, it isn't an ideal world. So think of the framework like a toolbox. Look at it if you are thinking about what needs to be done next, trying to discover what has gone wrong or if you want to work out how to tackle the next task.

Key actions		Task	Team	Individual
Define objectives		Identify tasks and constraints	Hold team meetings and share commitment	Clarify objectives Gain acceptance
Plan	Gather information	Consider options Check resources	Consult Develop suggestions	Encourage ideas Assess skills
	Decide	Priorities Timescales Standards	Structure	Allocate jobs Delegate Set targets
Brief		Clarify objectives Describe plan	Explain decisions Answer questions Check understanding	Listen Enthuse
Monitor Support		Co-ordinate Assess progress Maintain standards	Advise Reconcile conflict	Assist/reassure counsel/ discipline
			Recognize effort	
Evaluate		Summarize Review objectives Replan if necessary	Recognize and gain from success Learn from mistakes	Appraise performance
			Guide and train	Give praise

So action-centred leadership focuses on the *doing* part of being a leader. It gives you the basic skills that you need in order to get the job done, build a team and develop individuals. However, there is of course much more to being a leader than simply doing those three things. Nowadays, your team and your organization are going to expect a great deal more from you than just that. This is where we move on to the *being* part of leadership.

Liberating Leadership – the 'being' part of leadership

The Industrial Society conducted some research into how leadership has changed and what people believe makes an effective leader today.

The key element of the research is that it was conducted among the very same sort of people that you are going to be leading so it is probably fairly reflective of what your own team would say they wanted in a leader if you asked them.

Our research showed that people:

● want leaders not bosses
● want flat structures
● want everyone to take a lead when necessary
● want a responsive culture.

The survey also reported on what people felt were the characteristics and behaviours of good leaders. Good leaders:

● showed enthusiasm
● supported others
● recognized individual effort
● provided direction
● demonstrated personal integrity
● practised what they preached
● were fair
● encouraged team work
● had strong self-belief and believed in others.

Essentially in order for people to regard managers as leaders those managers need to:

● **L**iberate by freeing those closest to the job to take their own decisions

● **E**ncourage their staff and support them where necessary

● **A**chieve the purpose for which the team exists

● **D**evelop people and teams

● set an **E**xample by their own behaviour

● build **R**elationships on trust.

All of which makes a very handy mnemonic '**L E A D E R**' for you to remember.

As a result of this research, The Industrial Society has developed a model which aims to reflect what is needed in leaders today, incorporating the principles of action-centred leadership, but taking into account how the world has changed and what people want differently in leadership today from what they were happy to accept before.

There is a simple model to describe it:

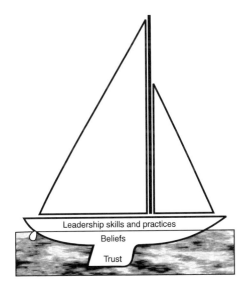

This is called the Leader Ship and is a visual representation of the two key elements of an effective leader. First, the bit above the line, the hull, is the 'above the line' leadership actions. This is the 'doing' part of being a leader, where you use all the skills and techniques of action-centred leadership. This is the bit that people see. In other words, the skills you exhibit when acting as a leader. Briefing people, walking the job, setting and maintaining standards, carrying out appraisals and so on.

The bit below the line, the keel, represents the 'being' part of being a leader. This is the bit that relates to who you are as a person, what your values and beliefs are, what you think about yourself and others. This is the part that others don't normally see, but which influences all of your actions and behaviours as a leader. However, the keel of the boat is the part that keeps the boat stable in the water, and is the part that is seen when there are storms tossing the boat about. The same is true when there are difficulties at work. That is the time when many people show their 'true colours'. When you can really see what their value and belief system is.

A combination of the 'doing' and 'being' elements makes up what we call the liberating leader.

The book *Liberating Leadership* says that liberating leaders:

1   Have a strong belief in their own and other people's capabilities and set out to release this latent power in others and themselves.
2   Enthuse their followers and put enthusiasm into whatever they do.
3   Act as protectors of others, i.e., they support their followers against attack from outside interests.
4   Through a process of tutoring and mentoring develop the self-esteem of followers such that they have the potential to become effective achievers or contributors themselves.
5   Manage by using an effective combination of direction, delegation and listening.
6   Enhance the worth of their followers by ensuring they are in tune with their environment and are producing effective outcomes.
7   Respect others and believe that they, given the opportunity, will contribute to the success of the organization through their own inner conviction and drive.
8   Personalize rather than generalize their leadership approach, in that they do not seek or use a single 'best practice' approach, but set out to create an empathetic relationship in which leader behaviour matches the needs of those being led.
9   Release the latent self-leadership capability of their followers,

i.e., they behave in ways that encourage their followers to take charge of their environment and take responsibility and accountability for their own actions.

10 Democratize hierarchical work environments by using the structures, processes and procedures to strengthen and enable followers rather than to control them.'

The key thing for you to note about this is that people really want their leaders to be human beings who act with honesty and integrity, live out their own values and respect the values of the people who work with and for them.

No one expects you to be perfect, but you do need to admit it openly when you are not and, above all, don't pretend that you don't make mistakes.

Why not ask your team what kind of leader they would like you to be. That will give you a framework to operate in. It certainly won't do any harm to your credibility as a leader to ask the people whom you are expected to lead what they need and expect of you. You are highly likely to find they list much the same things as we found.

'A good leader is also a good follower.' [American Proverb]

Summary and key actions

- Managers manage things, leaders lead people – management is about doing things right, leadership is about doing the right things.
- Be aware of who you are being as well as what you are doing.
- Demonstrate your values and live them with your team.
- Believe in your team and demonstrate your trust.
- Use the framework for leadership as a toolbox.

CHAPTER 4

Building relationships

The higher up the management ladder you climb, the more you will discover that the biggest part of the job is building and maintaining relationships.

It is widely acknowledged that the key to success for many people is their ability to influence others. Certainly, you will find that most very senior managers will agree that a large part of their time is spent building relationships: with customers, suppliers, their staff, their colleagues, their own directors, chairs of the board and so on.

But why? Why is this such a crucial part of the job? Well, if you think about it, it's fairly obvious. You need other people in order to get the job done; to buy your products and services; to agree to your proposals; to implement your decisions and so on. If people aren't willing to work hard for you and the organization then the job won't get done well, or in the worst case, it won't get done at all. Or your products/services won't be bought, your proposals will be rejected, your decisions don't get implemented.

Many people assume that you are either 'naturally' good with people or you are not and that's an end to it. Well, that may well be true, and I could get into the nature/nurture debate. However, I prefer to believe that you learn how to interact successfully with people when you are young and that you can learn new ways as you get older.

It is also worth remembering that as you change job roles in an organization from team worker to leader, your relationships will also change.

This is necessary and unavoidable and if you believe you can maintain your existing relationships within the team or the organization in the same way that you did before then you are in the wrong job. You cannot. Your professional relationship has changed from that of colleague to that of boss. This makes a big difference to how you need to handle relationships. For example, every comment you make about individuals within the team will be taken seriously by all who hear it. People know that you now have the ability to affect their jobs, whereas before you didn't so it probably didn't matter too much to them what you thought of them.

This is particularly challenging if you were promoted from within the team and have a friend who now reports to you.

In addition, you will no longer be able to moan about the boss to the team in the way you did before. Now you are part of the management, and every time you knock any manager, including your own, you are essentially knocking yourself. Whatever your personal views may be about them or their decisions you need to keep them to yourself.

Actually, and here's a bit that's quite difficult to get used to, your team will moan about you! Oh yes they will. No matter how hard you work to keep them happy, at some point you will make a decision that they won't like and you will be in for a hard time. Seriously, people do whinge about the boss. And, provided it's not destructive, then I think it's probably OK. It's healthy for people to have a good old moan occasionally. Your job is not so much to prevent them moaning, but to make sure that the moans aren't about serious problems that you haven't dealt with.

So, let's talk about relationships. What are good relationships? What do they look like and how do you achieve them?

Good relationships have many features in common, whether they are professional relationships at work, relationships with friends or relationships with family. Some of the common characteristics of a good relationship will probably include:

- both people trust each other
- both people tell each other the truth, tactfully and constructively where necessary
- both people like each other and enjoy each other's company
- both people understand the other person's motivations and respect their different values
- both people don't hold grudges
- both people are willing to say sorry and to accept the other person's apology
- both people accept that the other person will make mistakes and doesn't blame them for it
- both people will help each other out of a tight spot
- both people will make an effort to talk to each other
- both people will keep the other informed
- both people will admit when they have made a mistake
- both people will ask for and offer help
- both people can relax and have a joke with each other.

There are of course many more. And I expect you're looking at some of the list and thinking 'This may apply to my private life, but do I really have to like the people I work with?'. I'm sure you've heard people say that leaders don't have to be liked, they just have to be respected. Well, OK. But show me a leader who you can't stand but who you do respect. There may be some, but I'll bet there aren't many. It's often managers and trainers, probably in self defence, who say you don't need to be liked only respected!

We are, above all, human beings, with human fallibilities and it is very difficult to put a lot of effort into working for some one you don't like. Actually, there are very few people I have met who I don't like at some level. Even if they're not someone I would choose for my best friend, I can usually find something likeable about them. I find it really difficult to work with people I don't like and I will tend to avoid having to work with them if possible. As a professional, I do what I need to do for them, but I rarely push the boat out. Does that make me an awful human being? Maybe, but I suspect I'm just normal, like the rest of you. I find that looking for things to like in people actually helps me to do my job.

There are three main areas of importance when I talk about building relationships. First, how to create relationships using certain techniques, second, how to network within your organization and outside it, and third, how to keep a relationship even when there is conflict using effective negotiating and influencing skills. All of the points below affect each of these three areas.

Furthermore, all of the points I am going to make are equally valid whether you are dealing with a customer, a member of your own team, a colleague or your boss.

Will you be my friend?

What makes people think you are a good listener? What makes people think you are good to be around? What makes people tell you things? What makes people like you? It's actually very, very straightforward. People want to be understood. All people, everywhere.

People want you to see them not from your perspective but from theirs. A friend of mine says that 'people judge others by their actions and themselves by their motives'. Someone who is good with people always looks beyond the surface to see what has motivated someone to behave in a particular way. And does so without judging.

So how do you get to understand people? What you need to do is listen to them. Listen properly, deeply and from their point of view, not your own.

Listening is an interesting phenomenon. We get taught how to read, how to write and how to speak. But no one teaches us how to listen and yet I would say that it is a vital skill.

We listen with the three Es. Our Ears, our Eyes and our Emotions. None of our listening happens in a vacuum. We bring to all of our listening our own hopes, fears, learning, prejudices, preconceptions, values and so on. We hear people through a 'filter' of who we are. That means that we never really 'get' who *they* are, the most we ever get is who *we think* they are. Anais Nin said 'We don't listen to things as they are, we listen to things as we are.'

For example, have you ever been listening to a speaker at a course or on a conference whom you really didn't like? For one reason or another, maybe because they used sexist or racist language, or they were dismissive of something you support, or because they simply spoke very boringly and monotonously, you found that you stopped listening to them. Or it might be a member of your team having a whinge and you find it hard to listen.

It is very easy to think that if other people want us to listen then they have to talk in a way that makes us want to listen. It is true to a certain extent that the most effective communicators are those who make their 'audience' want to listen to them. However, I think that most people aren't brilliant communicators and, even if they are, it's probably not all the time. Of course, you need to make sure that when you speak you are trying to do it in a way that makes people want to listen. However, the problem is that as soon as you expect other people to make you want to listen you are going to lose out on an awful lot of useful information, simply because you didn't like the way in which it was being said. As soon as you stop listening, you are the loser not the speaker. Because the speaker already knows what they know, so they have nothing to lose. You don't know what they know and as soon as you stop listening you never will.

It's really best to put yourself aside when you are listening. That way you are more likely to be genuinely listening.

Most of us listen in a particular way, which is illustrated by the following simple model.

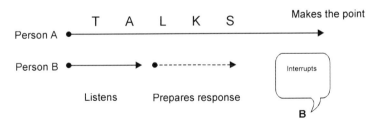

As you can see from the model most of us listen to the first part of what someone is saying, then we start preparing our response and then we interrupt, very often before the person has made their point. The interruption is not necessarily a verbal one, it can simply be an interruption in our head in that we have moved on in our thoughts from what they are saying to us.

The point is, this is a very unconscious process and we all engage in it. Whenever you are talking to people this is what will be happening to their listening. There are some things you can do as the speaker to help minimize this, which I will cover in the communication chapter. For the purposes of this chapter, however, I want to concentrate on what you can do to overcome it in yourself.

How to be a good listener – 5 easy steps

1   **Listen to understand**. This means suspending your own thought and judgements and really listening to what the person is actually saying and what underlies it. Ask questions for clarification, not to 'test' or catch people out. And above all, be honest. If you can't see why they have said what they have, that's probably not because they are wrong or stupid. It's because you still haven't understood. So you haven't listened enough. By the way, understanding doesn't necessarily mean agreeing. You can understand something and completely disagree with it.

    One of the most useful sayings I know is *'Seek first to understand, before being understood'*.

2   **When listening, separate the person from the point**. In other words, whether you disagree or agree with them, it will be about the point they are making, not who they are. You can completely value a person and still disagree profoundly with them. I know a homophobic individual – who is still a close friend, even though I disagree with their attitude towards homosexuality. I value the person, even though I don't value their position. You just need to make it clear that although you don't support the point you still support the person.

3   **Be aware of their body language**. People say so much without using words and sometimes it is easier, particularly when you are under pressure, to ignore very obvious signs that they are unhappy with something. You don't necessarily need any training to understand body language. We are all good at reading body language, we do it all the time.

The problem occurs when we pretend that we haven't noticed it so that we don't have to deal with it. You know the sort of thing I mean, being aware that someone doesn't agree with something that's been said in a meeting because of the way they are sitting and the expression on their face, but because of pressures of time thinking 'Well, if they really have a problem they'll say something'. Of course, the consequence of that is that they don't say anything, but they also don't do what we wanted them to because they didn't agree and we didn't help them to say so.

Never let negative body language go un-noticed. Say, 'Clare, you look puzzled. Can I clarify?'. Or 'Judy, you seem to disagree with that statement. What's the problem?'. Or 'Justin, was there anything you wanted to add to what's been said so far?'. Nine times out of ten people do want you to notice and invite them to speak. So – notice and invite them to speak.

4 **Be aware of your own prejudices** as you are listening. It's naive to think you don't have any. All of us have prejudices in one way or another. The skill is to recognize when you are acting or thinking out of prejudice and not out of common sense or objectivity. A truly good listener doesn't claim not to have prejudices or preconceptions, but tries to overcome them by recognizing them, labelling them 'blind prejudice' and putting them to one side.

5 **Be generous in your listening**. People don't always say the right thing in the right way. They don't always appeal to us. We don't always like the way they look. They will also make mistakes in the things they say. They may say something that we disagree with. They may sound arrogant, or patronizing or frankly simply boring. However, they will probably still have something useful to say if we really listen. Essentially, try not to let your feelings about someone affect your listening to them. Whether you like them or not doesn't change their message or who they are. Allow that people are human beings when they are talking to you and listen to what they are trying to say, not to your feelings about them as a person.

If you only get one thing from this book, I want it to be the crucial importance of listening. And you also need to remember that you will never be a perfect listener. The most you can do is keep trying.

Actually, in my experience managers are often the worst listeners. The fact that they have ambition to be managers often means they have something they want to say or do and so they are less likely to be good listeners. That's OK. It just means you and I have to work slightly harder at it than others. However, it's really worth the effort.

So the first and most important thing in order to build relationships is to listen to and understand the other person. Following is a list of the 10 things that you can do to build relationships with others.

1 Listen
Remember – listen to understand; separate the person from the point; be aware of body language; be aware of your own prejudices and be generous in your listening.

2 Make time for them
This doesn't mean dropping everything on the spot necessarily, but it does mean telling people when you will make time for them and sticking to it. It also means being available. And watch this one. I have a colleague who says she is always available for people. And, of course, in her own mind, she is. She certainly never turns anyone away. The problem is that she always looks so stressed that no one wants to bother her or add to her burden so they don't go to her with problems or mistakes. You need always to welcome people with a smile even if the world is tumbling around you.

3 Notice what they do
Whether an individual is a colleague, a member of your team, a manager or the person who cleans the front steps of the building, make an effort to notice what they do. The simple thing to do to show that you have noticed is to ask questions and listen to the answer.

I had a manager who used to ask me at least once a week how the job was going and how I was. Now, I don't know about you, but I'm one of those irritating people who want to answer those kinds of questions in some depth. So I used to tell him. Unfortunately, it was usually very apparent within a few minutes that his mind had moved on and he wasn't really listening to the answer. He knew he had to ask, because that's what managers do. He obviously hadn't realized that he was also supposed to listen to the answer. I always knew he wasn't really all that interested in what I did. It also made it hard for me to care about what I did.

4 Praise

Seek to praise people for what they do. It is easy to remember to praise people who perform out of the ordinary tasks or who make some extra effort. But there are a lot of people out there who are just doing a very good job at what is expected of them and no one ever notices it or praises them. I sometimes lead a residential programme at Balliol College, Oxford. There is a woman there who hoovers the conference offices that we use. I remember one time, it was about six-thirty in the morning and I happened to bump in to her. I thanked her for doing the hoovering, praised her for the good job she did and told her what a difference it made to the rest of my team to come in to an office that looked clean and tidy. It was easy for me to say, it was true and I subsequently forgot all about it. The next morning, imagine my surprise to see her there, moving all the furniture to make sure she hoovered behind it. She'd also brought along a cloth and duster to have a quick wipe of the skirting board. Just because I had said well done. Whom have you praised lately?

5 Communicate

I cover more of this in Chapter 7, however, you must make the time to let people know what's going on, what decisions have been made, how things are going, etc. And most of all, make the time to communicate *face to face*. But more about that later.

6 Accept mistakes

We all make mistakes. Sometimes the mistakes are because of stupidity or carelessness. People who say they don't blame people for mistakes unless they are stupid or careless are not being realistic. We are all stupid and careless sometimes. Certainly I am. That doesn't mean that you don't hold people responsible for mistakes or that you don't expect them to fix their mistakes, but it does means that you let go of the matter once the mistake has been acknowledged and dealt with. And you continue to trust that person with the same thing that they made the mistake with. If you take a job away from someone because they made a mistake or stop trusting them, then you are into 'blame'. It is very difficult to trust them again because you feel let down.

As a manager, however, it is not for others to prove that you can trust them, it's for you to carry on trusting them, even when they make mistakes, just as you want your own manager to do the same for you. Really good leaders prove they are capable of trust, not that people are trustworthy.

7   Be open and act out of integrity

Being open means letting people see who you are as a person quite apart from your job. It also means being open to them, letting them feel that they can trust you with things about themselves as humans, quite apart from being part of your team or your manager or your colleague. Acting out of integrity means being honest. Being honest is not just about not telling lies, it is about saying what needs to be said and being true to your own values.

8   Offer support

Actively look for ways in which you can help people. If help is asked for, look to say yes first. Only say no if you really can't help, but always help them to find someone who can. Offer help if you can see someone might need it. This includes people not in your own team.

9   Make time to be social

One of the best ways to get to know people and therefore to build relationships is to take time to chat informally with them. This means taking time to find out what they do in their spare time, what their likes and dislikes are, what their lives are like. Attend social functions at work and make the effort to network. Go for a drink if you are invited. Take the time to chat at the coffee machine. Ten minutes of what appears to be 'idle' chat can save you days of work if you need to phone that person to help you out one day! We find it easier to push out the boat for people we have a relationship with than for those we don't, regardless of what we ought to do professionally.

10 Be yourself

Don't pretend to be what you are not. Show people who you really are, warts and all. You are a great human being with big strengths, and probably big weaknesses. This means being honest about your mistakes, laughing at yourself and bringing your whole self to work.

Summary and key actions

- Listen without judging.
- Listen to understand.
- Make time for people.
- Remember that people will see you differently now that you are a manager.
- Be generous in your listening.

CHAPTER 5

Networking and managing relationships when there is conflict

Networking is a very important part of being a manager. Part of your responsibility to your team and the organization is to know people and be known. This means both people within the organization and outside.

Networking is the very simple process of getting to know people with whom you wouldn't come into contact during the normal course of your day or week.

The purpose of networking is to build relationships and share knowledge. Sometimes there is a very specific reason to network in that you want to promote your organization, but mostly networking is about building relationships with people who are valuable to know.

Networking also enables you to fulfil some of your personal or work goals, help others to achieve theirs (it's never one-way if it's effective networking), raise your profile and that of your organization or team/department.

Networking doesn't have to be a formal activity. Certainly, some of your networks will be formed because you join a club with the express purpose of networking. However, more often networking occurs simply because you have joined a club or group that enables you to meet new people or because you take the time to get to know people at social and other events.

Eve Warren and Caroline Gielnick in their book *Empower Yourself* give some very useful tips on how to network effectively. Here are a few:

What to do	External networking	Internal networking
1 Be clear about what you want	Go into networking knowing what it is you want to achieve and being clear about what it it is you have to offer.	Same as external, but remember you are likely to come across these people in the context of work as well.
2 Approach people first	This is the really hard bit and the bit I hate the most. However, most of us feel uncomfortable in situations where we don't know anyone – even seemingly the most confident people. Simply start by introducing yourself and then ask about the other person. Get them talking by asking why they are there, what they hope to achieve, etc.	This is particularly important internally because it helps your colleagues to see that you are keen to get to know them. The skills are exactly the same as for external except you can ask them more directly about their job and how long they have worked for the organization. You can also ask what they like about it most and least. Very useful to know!
3 Give a firm handshake	This sound a bit obvious, but you'd be amazed how many people don't do this.	As for external.
4 Introduce positively	Speak positively about who you are and what you do. Don't simply say you work for such and such organization – they may not have heard of it and may feel uncomfortable about asking. Say who you are, what your organization does (which is, after all, more important than the name) and what your role is within it.	This also applies if you are networking internally. Don't assume that just because people work for the same organization as you they necessarily know what it is your team/department do, or who you are.

What to do	External networking	Internal networking
5 Make the conversation two-way	I've said the most important thing is to find out about the other person. This is true. However, it is also important to make sure that they have connected with you and that means sharing a little about yourself also. Just don't monopolize the conversation.	It will be tempting during internal networking to get into gossip. It's best to avoid it because you don't want to be labelled a gossip at the early stages of your new role as a manager. Or at any stage of your career for that matter.
6 Exchange business cards	Always take business cards with you to courses, conferences and other events so that you can give them to people. If you get given them it's a good idea to make a quick note on the back of who the person was and what you spoke about. It's very easy to forget if you meet a lot of people.	Find a way to fix the person in your memory. A quick note to yourself made after you've met them is a good way. You don't want to bump into them again and forget who they are.
7 Circulate	Don't stay with the same person for the whole event. Make sure you meet as many people as possible without making any conversations so short as to be meaningless. If you don't want to appear rude, then take the person you are talking to with you to meet others. The main point is not to waste the opportunity to meet as many people as possible.	This is equally important for internal networking and probably easier to do because you can ask the person you are talking to if they know anyone from, e.g., accounts, because you'd like to meet them.
8 Maintain contact after the event	If you have met people with whom you really want to maintain contact, make sure you write them a note afterwards, saying how much you enjoyed meeting them. It makes it a lot easier to keep in touch.	A quick phone call is probably better for an internal network. It seems more natural.

Managing relationships when there is conflict

The real test of the strength of your relationships with your team, your colleagues, your customers, suppliers and your own manager is how you handle things when there is conflict or disagreement. And there will always be conflict of some kind or another.

To deal with conflict use interpersonal skills, in particular assertiveness. Assertiveness is about win/win. This means that whatever the outcome of the situation, both parties feel OK about themselves as people, even if the outcome for either of them is not what they wanted. Assertiveness does not mean getting your own point across at the expense of others. If you have truly acted assertively you will have listened to the other person's point of view and understood it. Good interpersonal and assertive skills are such an important part of being a good leader and an effective manager that I strongly advise you to get some training in it.

To distinguish the characteristics (verbal, thoughts, actions and

Characteristic	Aggressive	Passive	Assertive
Thought	I'm better than I'm right You have a problem	I'm not good enough I don't deserve I have a problem	We're both important We're equal We both have a problem
Words	You make me angry Who are you to say? Who do you think you are?	I can't I'm sorry I'm not very good	I believe we can Let's talk about it What do you think?
Actions	Shouting and looking to blame Slamming doors	Speaking weakly and trying to avoid blame Silence	Speaking calmly and trying to identify the problem Asking questions to seek clarification
Values	Out to win	Trying to avoid blame	Focus on the problem to be solved

values) of assertiveness from passiveness and aggression I have adapted the simple table on p.50, from *Get a Life!* by Bede Cammock-Elliott, and added a few extra thoughts of my own.

As a manager you are now in a unique position when it comes to managing your behaviour and this means that you need to ensure that you behave assertively and seek win/win whenever possible.

To deal with conflict follow this checklist before entering any conversation where there is likely to be conflict:

- **Identify what you are trying to achieve out of the communication**. First, are you sure that your facts are right? You will need to make sure that you allow them to speak first and tell you their side of the story. What is the outcome you want? Do you want to let off steam? Resolve the situation? Let somebody know how you feel? Punish someone? It is really important that you are clear about the outcome you want, because this is going to affect what behaviour you choose in order to achieve it. You must always remember the long term consequences of any action you choose to take. For example, if someone has made a mistake and you don't want them to make it again then the last thing you should do is tell them off. That way, they will be afraid to admit future mistakes and may end up hiding something that could be more important. Letting off steam may make you feel better in the short term, but could have disastrous consequences in the long term.

- **Imagine what their reaction is likely to be**. Try to imagine how they may respond to what you have to say. What may seem logical and reasonable to you will not necessarily seem so to them.

- **Decide how you might respond if the reaction is different from the one you want**. Think about what to do, for example, if they get angry. Or if they completely disagree with what you are saying.

- **Think about other ways of achieving your objective**. Approaching them directly might lead to a confrontation which neither of you wants. Do you need to talk to them outside of the work environment? Is this issue important enough to deal with in this way? Can it be brought up at a one-to-one?

- **Choose the best time and place to approach people.** Think about the timing of your conversation. You want to be able to be honest with each other. If the other person is feeling afraid or hassled, or if they are conscious of other people being around, you won't get the best result.
- **Have a 'fallback' position.** You will not always get exactly the outcome you are looking for, especially at the first conversation. What will you do if this is the case?
- **Decide your limits in advance.** How far are you prepared to compromise? What are your limits? What happens if you find out something during the course of the conversation that you didn't expect to hear? What are you going to do if you and the other person cannot resolve the conflict?

The important thing to remember is the language you choose when dealing with conflict. Always give the other person a chance to explain their view of things first. And make sure that you listen.

Below are some examples of situations you might have to deal with, with some things to remember.

Information gathering

- Explain why you need the information
- Avoid over-justification
- Ask open questions
- Do not interrupt
- Give appropriate non-verbal responses
- Do not respond verbally to every statement the other person makes.

Information giving

- State your objectives
- Be direct and to the point
- Avoid over-justification
- Summarize and point the way ahead.

Disagreeing

- Clearly identify areas of agreement and disagreement
- Support your ideas with objective evidence if possible

- Avoid personalizing your disagreement
- Disagree with what is said, not with the person who is saying it
- Be prepared to change your mind
- Negotiate a positive solution.

Making requests

- Be direct and to the point
- Explain why you are making the request
- Don't apologize for asking
- Keep it short and simple
- Avoid manipulation. Let the request stand on its own merits
- Avoid personalizing the request
- Be prepared for the other person to say no.

Refusing requests

- Briefly and clearly state what you are willing and unwilling to do
- Avoid making profuse apologies
- Offer an explanation but avoid over-justification
- Keep it short and simple
- Avoid personalizing your refusal
- If pressed, repeat your refusal, slowing down and stressing important words.

Responding to confrontation

- Acknowledge the strength of the other person's feelings
- Acknowledge their needs
- State your needs
- Review the facts and options in an attempt to resolve the issue
- Summarize and point the way ahead.

Most of all, remember that your team and the people you work with will look to you to set an example of how to deal with people constructively. If you are not confident in dealing with conflict ask for some training or coaching.

Building and making the most of relationships with other departments

Every single department in an organization is vital to the running of that organization. Your relationship with other departments is very important. You need other departments in order to be able to carry out your own team/department's function. For example, you need the accounts department to pay the invoices, and you need the personnel department, if you have one, to pay the wages. You need the post room to deliver the post, the cleaners to clean up and so on.

There is a psychology of organizations. Organizations take on a 'character', an identity, both internally and to the outside world. For example, you could probably quite easily describe the identity and characteristics of organizations like Virgin Atlantic Airways, Woolworths, your bank, etc.

What is particularly interesting about organizations having an identity is that people will often attribute that identity to all the individuals within that organization. If we perceive the organization as being young and modern, we will expect all the people from it that we meet to have those same characteristics. If we perceive the organization as old fashioned and behind the times, we will attribute those same values to all the people who work there. Think of a time when you had a bad experience with a shop or restaurant. We rarely think that it's just one person at fault. Normally, we won't go back and give another employee from that organization a chance to prove that they're not really that bad.

Our expectation of their behaviour has two consequences. First, it means that we will treat them accordingly. Second, it means that we will expect them to respond in a certain way.

The same thing occurs within organizations. Certain departments take on certain 'personalities' or identities. Every organization, even the most fluid and flexible, organizes itself in departments or teams, normally by function. So accounts is one function, sales may be another, and so on. And each different function is seen in a different way.

Desmond Morris in *The Human Zoo* talks about people who identify with each other and have similar values forming themselves into tribes which then form a common culture. Well, exactly the same thing happens in the workplace. And people in a tribe will adopt common forms of dress, language, behaviour, even though they still may maintain their individuality. Have a look at how people dress in different parts of your organization. I bet you find that each department, with probably some exceptions, has people dressing in a very similar way.

You'll probably also find that they adopt their own 'language' in the form of jargon that they use. This is mostly jargon which is only comprehensible to those in the team/department or 'tribe'. They will also adopt 'in jokes' and a common set of behaviours and habits which will bind them together as a group and exclude others.

The main thing to note here is that this is perfectly normal and we all do it. So you need to recognize and understand that this is how we will all behave. What it also means is that you will defend and support your 'culture' to any external person, even if you don't necessarily support it yourself within the team.

Your job is to overcome this natural resistance both in your own and other departments, in a way which allows each of you to retain your identity/culture, but has you working together co-operatively.

Begin by establishing what you want to achieve from your relationships with other departments or teams. It will vary in the specifics, but is likely to have common factors, like achieving results, having good, helpful relationships, and so on.

Look at the image of your own department. How are you perceived by others? Can you find out by asking them? Then establish what kind of image you would like your team to have. Get your own team to identify how they would like to be seen by others. Identify some common ideas, for example:

- saying yes to requests
- meeting deadlines
- being honest
- not complaining about other departments
- taking responsibility for problems
- thinking about how you speak to people in other departments
- use of jargon – learning theirs and not using yours
- not blaming or accusing when things go wrong – but concentrating on how to get the result or solve the problem.

On the whole, people will let things that have happened in the past colour how they see you and your team in the future. When I was first a supervisor, I worked for an organization where it was traditional to take new people around when they first joined and introduce them to other departments. The idea was that you would greet the new person in your department and give a 10-minute introduction to what your department did and so on. Protocol said that you would phone the supervisor of the other departments and let them know who you were bringing and what time you would arrive.

On one particular occasion, one of my fellow supervisors, Helen, whom I didn't know particularly well, brought around a new member of staff. Unfortunately, she had completely forgotten to ring me to tell me she was coming. Furthermore, it was the end of the month and I was frantically trying to produce the end of month figures. So along came Helen with her new team member. 'Hello Debra,' she said, 'this is Margaret, would you mind telling her a bit about your department?'. Well, I was really irritated by this. 'Helen,' I said, somewhat acidly, 'you didn't ring to tell me you were coming and you know you're supposed to. I'm really busy, it's the end of month as you well know, so I can't spare very much time. It'll have to be quick.' Helen gave me a somewhat tight smile and I gave a quick rundown about the department and they then left.

Needless to say, I never had a good relationship with Helen after this encounter. Because, despite the fact that I had a point, I behaved appallingly. I humiliated her in front of her new member of staff. That is very hard to forgive. I could have been flexible, but I wasn't.

The moral of the story is that other people and other departments make mistakes. They ignore the rules and forget to do things 'properly', especially when they are busy. And so do we. You need to be flexible, and talk about how to avoid mistakes next time, not point out how useless they are. And if you do that for them, there is a greater chance that they will be more flexible for you and your team when you get it wrong.

It is important to recognize that we don't help strangers in the same way that we help our friends. So, a really key action for you is to get to know people in other departments. Some of the principles here are similar to those I touched on when I talked about networking. However, here are some more things that you could do:

- understand what their priorities are and help them to understand yours
- find out what their problems are
- visit them in their own departments
- make them feel welcome when they come to you – stop work, look up and offer help – or offer them coffee and a chat
- get to know them as individuals even if it's only on the phone
- explain your problems
- don't justify when you make mistakes – admit them
- offer help
- ask for help when you need it
- always negotiate when asking for things – don't demand.

An organization is a bit like a soccer team, in which every player has their own responsibility. They know what they are supposed to do. However, they all know that the whole team's aim is to win the game. So, if a defender scores a goal, when they're not supposed to because it's the job of the forwards, you don't hear the team saying to the referee, 'You should disallow that goal because he/she shouldn't have scored it'. Similarly, if one of the players is in difficulty, the other players don't leave them to it, saying, 'Not my problem, it's not my job to defend the goal'. Maybe if organizations thought of themselves more like a soccer team there would be less destructive inter-departmental competition.

At the end of the day, you are one organization and every team within it needs to be successful so that the whole organization wins. It's pointless standing on one end of a sinking ship, looking down at the other end, saying to yourself, 'I'm all right'. If any end of the ship goes down – you'll go down with it.

Summary and key actions

- Make an effort to build up both internal and external networks.

- When dealing with conflict think about your objective – not your immediate gratification.
- In conflict situations always allow others to explain their point of view.
- Take time to understand the problems and priorities of other departments.
- Concentrate on getting the result not apportioning blame.

CHAPTER 6

Motivation

'May I ask whether these pleasing attentions proceed from the impulse of the moment or are the result of previous study?' [Jane Austen, *Pride and Prejudice* (1813)]

One of the biggest challenges you will face as a manager is creating a team of motivated people. Motivation is what makes a person want to do something. And the key word here is *want*. There are things that we all have to do that we may not want to. Motivation is when people give willingly. You can always *make* people do things but to have them feel motivated is quite different. A simple definition of motivation in the work context is *'Getting people to do willingly and well those things that need to be done'*.

Ned Herrmann, in *The Whole Brain Business Book,* talks about how you cannot motivate people, they can only motivate themselves. As he says, 'The facts of the matter are that we all motivate ourselves. This inner self-motivation can be encouraged in a number of ways by supervisors, managers and executives'. It is becoming increasingly obvious that the most you can do as a manager is remove the barriers to motivation and create an environment in which people are able to motivate themselves. More on this later.

It is quite easy to distinguish people who are motivated from people who are not. There is also a distinction between being unmotivated and de-motivated. Unmotivated people have no desire to do a particular task. De-motivated people did have the desire to do it, but have lost that motivation. In my experience it is easier to re-motivate those who are de-motivated than it is to inspire motivation in people who really have no interest in doing the task in the first place.

Possible characteristics of motivated, de-motivated and unmotivated people

Motivated	De-motivated	Unmotivated
Asks questions for clarification	Asks rhetorical questions which are unanswerable	Doesn't ask questions
Seeks to solve problems	Points problems out to others	Ignores problems
Wants to share knowledge with others	Wants to complain about difficulties to others	Doesn't talk about the task/job at all
Puts in the time to get the job	Wastes time	Does the bare minimum to get the job done
Is generally quick to respond to requests	Responds to requests reluctantly	Forgets they have been asked
Seeks to help others	Can't help others and doesn't ask for help themselves	Doesn't occur to them that they might need or offer help
Generally seems positive	Generally seems negative	Neither positive nor negative because they are disengaged from the task
More likely to cope with things going wrong with good humour	More likely to over-react to things going wrong or complain about them	Doesn't care if things go wrong
Positive attitude to problems – I can sort this out	Negative attitude to problems – doesn't think they can sort the problem	May generally be positive, just not interested in this particular job

Motivation is an interesting subject. There are many theories about what motivates people, and all of them have some value. The key thing is to make them work in practice. To learn how to create an environment in which people can help to motivate themselves, you first need to have some understanding of what makes people 'tick'. People, despite having a lot in common, also have very specific individual differences. There are generic commonalities of values and motivation and yet each individual finds a different stimulation. I want to cover some of the very basic theories of motivation before turning to what you can do practically as a manager to unlock motivation in your team.

Understanding people

There are many different theories about what makes people tick. Many theories of personality are linked to motivation, although the emphasis they place on it varies. All of this knowledge is useful to us in attempting to understand what motivates people. However, for the most part, one theory alone doesn't provide the whole answer and so an overall understanding of different theories can help to inform our actions and our thinking when we are trying to release motivation in others.

One theory by H. Eysenck says that people have three personality dimensions – extraversion-introversion, neuroticism-stability and psychoticism. Essentially this theory says that people's personalities are linked to their biological make up and there's not much anyone can do to change them. In other words, you are born extravert or introvert, etc.

Another theory is that people act as scientists in that they form a theory about how the world works and then test out the theory. That is, our personalities are formed by what happens to us. So we take each experience, process it and use it to make judgements about future experiences. This theory says that fundamentally people's motivation is based on their need to predict their environment and thereby reduce uncertainty and increase mastery over the world.

Yet another theory is that people have personality traits which help them to have predictable behaviour. Personality grows and changes and people have the potential to become something different. Personality is formed by present circumstances, motives and conscious experiences.

All of this is useful information when thinking about what actions we can take to help motivate people.

Maslow's Hierarchy of Needs

These kinds of thinking encouraged Maslow, who was one of the founder members of the American Association for Humanistic Psychology, to publish a theory of motivation in 1954 which is still widely accepted as relevant today, particularly in the world of work. He called it the hierarchy of needs. He identified four kinds of basic human needs which he termed 'deficiency needs'. Deficiency needs are those needs which can

Maslow's Hierarchy of Needs

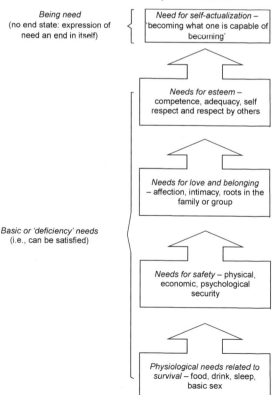

Being need
(no end state: expression of need an end in itself)

Need for self-actualization – 'becoming what one is capable of becoming'

Needs for esteem – competence, adequacy, self respect and respect by others

Needs for love and belonging – affection, intimacy, roots in the family or group

Basic or 'deficiency' needs
(i.e., can be satisfied)

Needs for safety – physical, economic, psychological security

Physiological needs related to survival – food, drink, sleep, basic sex be satisfied. He then identified a fifth and highest kind of need, which is only identified when the other four needs have been satisfied. That is the need for what he termed 'self-actualization'.

Self-actualization relates to an individual's need to achieve their potential but, Maslow argued, they would be unable to do this until the other four deficiency needs are satisfied.

So what does this mean for you? Well, if your team feel insecure, are worrying about how to pay the bills, then they are unlikely to be motivated to develop themselves or improve the quality of tasks. If they feel isolated from the rest of the team they are less likely to be motivated. If they feel that they are not cared about or not respected, they will not be so well motivated. And all of those four deficiency needs are something that you as a manager can do something about. They concern environment, pay, health and safety, being part of a team (which I will touch on later) and being respected.

Psychologist Carl Rogers talked about the conditions for personal growth. He said that people are dynamic and goal directed. Essentially people have two ways of identifying their own concept of who they are. First, their own experiences of what they can and cannot do, and second, evaluations of them made by other people. People have a need for unconditional regard, i.e., to be liked for themselves, regardless of what they do.

So, for you, this means you need to think about how you see your team and how you are treating them. Do they feel valued by you? Do they feel that you care about them as individuals as well as about the work they do for you? Do you give them the opportunity to test themselves, to try out new ways of doing things? Do you give them positive and helpful feedback about their behaviour and their actions?

This work, in particular the work of Maslow, was taken further by Douglas Macgregor. He talked about his theory of motivation at work in terms of Theory X and Theory Y. The two theories are representations of assumptions that people, in particular managers, may make about people with whom they work. Theory X assumes that people basically dislike work and need to be directed and controlled in order to produce results. Theory Y says that people like work and, under the right conditions, will seek to take responsibility for it.

Attitudes to work (the X-Y theory)

Theory X	Theory Y
1 People dislike work and will avoid it if they can	1 Work is necessary to people's psychological growth
2 People must be forced or bribed to make the right effort	2 People want to be interested in their work and under the right conditions they can enjoy it
3 People would rather be directed than accept responsibilities	3 People will direct themselves towards an accepted target
	4 People will seek and accept responsibility under the right conditions
	5 The discipline people impose on themselves is more effective, and can be more severe, than any imposed on them
4 People are motivated mainly by money	
5 People are motivated by anxiety about their security	6 Under the right conditions, people are motivated by the desire to realize their own potential
6 Most people have little creativity – except when getting around management rules	7 Creativity and ingenuity are widely distributed and grossly under-used

Research has shown that 'As managers have found, Theory Y, like Theory X, can be a self-fulfilling prophecy. By putting high expectations on people it often brings out the best in them. It thus shares the quality which marks out many of the theories of humanistic psychology – that by redefining the human situation it creates an opening for growth and becomes a force for change.' (Knight, 1982, p35 *Introduction to Psychology*)

What this means for you is that if you treat people as if they are competent, creative, energetic individuals who desire to grow and change, it is likely that that is how they will behave. If you treat them as if they are incompetent, whingey shirkers, then they are more likely to behave that way.

If you apply Theory X, you will of course get a result. You can certainly make people move. However, if what you want is real commitment and top quality results, then only Theory Y will produce that. A simple analogy is that of kicking a dog. If a dog is in your way and you kick it, it will move. But it will only move as far as you have kicked it and no further. However, the next time it is in your way, when you go to kick it, it may bite you. If, on the other hand, you train it properly, it will move enthusiastically and stay put.

How do you create the environment in which people can motivate themselves?

Hopefully, the theories you have read about above will have begun to give you a better understanding of what makes people behave in particular ways. Now the question is, with all that knowledge, what can you do in order to create the right environment for your team so that they will be motivated to a high degree?

The four simple things to do are:

- create the right environment
- communicate
- provide opportunities
- recognize and reward achievement.

Create the right environment

This is about making sure that people have the right equipment and resources to do the job and that their basic needs are satisfied, as per Maslow's hierarchy. Once these are satisfied, people will be freer to develop and grow.

- Is the kind of work that they are being asked to do boring and repetitive? Do you seek to make the work as interesting as possible?
- Do the team have the equipment they need to do the job?
- Do they have adequate resources?
- How is the team sitting? Are they ergonomically efficient?
- Are the 'right' people located close to each other?
- Do they all have job descriptions which clearly lay out their responsibilities?
- Are they aware of their standards of performance?
- Do they know how performance in their jobs impacts on others within the team and the rest of the organization?
- Have you helped them to create good relationships with others within the team and the organization to enable them to do their jobs properly?

Communicate

Communication is an important skill for helping with motivation and I will cover it in some detail in Chapter 7. Meanwhile, here are points that are specific to motivation.

- Do you have regular team meetings to up-date on progress?
- Do you have regular one-to-ones where you talk to the individual about their own work?
- Does everybody understand the objectives of the department and their own job?
- Do they know how they are doing, as individuals and against targets set?
- Do they have the opportunity to raise issues and ideas and are those issues and ideas listened to and acted upon?

Provide opportunities

People will feel motivated if they feel they are being given the opportunity to develop themselves, to grow as individuals and to extend their skills and expertise, both in the current job and for future possibilities.

- Have you set standards and targets for all members of the team?

● Do you delegate?
● Are you providing on and off the job training?
● Are you using team members who have expertise in something to share that expertise with others?
● Are you structuring work so that people are able to do what they are good at and enjoy doing?
● Do you structure work so that people have new challenges?
● Do you encourage membership of projects?
● Do you encourage team members to seek further or higher education to support them in their work or career development?

Recognize and reward achievement

When we think about recognition, what we tend to think of is monetary reward. Money certainly has a part to play in motivation. If people feel they are being paid a fair wage for the job, on the whole it won't motivate them particularly. They won't come bouncing into work because they're getting a decent wage. However, if they don't feel they are getting a fair wage they will almost certainly feel very de-motivated. Herzberg did a piece of research trying to investigate what motivates people at work (given that they were already being paid a decent wage). His survey showed that the two top-rated factors that led to the highest levels of motivation among people were achievement and recognition.

Recognition doesn't necessarily mean giving people huge increases in salary, although, of course, that is one way of recognizing achievement. Neither does the term 'reward' always have to apply to money. There are many ways of rewarding people without giving them money. For example:

● tell individuals face to face when they have done a good job
● get your line manager to send a note to the individual praising them
● mention good achievements at team meetings
● send a written note to their home and put it on file
● go out for team lunches
● buy cakes
● give or recommend pay rises

- give or recommend promotions
- allow people to take on the next challenging task
- give them time off
- give them more responsibility
- tell other people in front of them how good they are.

Above all, make plenty of use of praise. Praise is so easy to give and so often forgotten. Do remember the four Rs of praising people:

1 Real – don't say something is good if it isn't.
2 Relevant – general remarks like 'you're doing a good job' aren't terribly helpful, you need to be specific.
3 Regular – don't let praise be so rare that people remark 'the only pat on the back you get around here is if you lie face down under a cow!'.
4 Repeated – don't just praise the individual directly, make sure that you tell lots of other people that someone has done a good job.

Be aware that people won't feel motivated all the time, and sometimes their lack of motivation will be because of other factors outside work, about which you can usually do nothing.

Summary and key actions

- Think about your assumptions about people – how do you treat them?
- Make people feel as safe in their employment as you can while providing challenging work for them to do.
- Create the right environment for people.
- Provide opportunities for people.
- Praise – remember the four Rs.

CHAPTER 7

Communication

'Helen: *"What were you lecturing on in India?"*
Patterson: "Harold Pinter and the failure of communication."
Helen: "How did it go?"
Patterson: "I don't know. They didn't seem to understand a word I said."'

[Malcolm Bradbury and Christopher Bigsby, *The After Dinner Game*, BBC TV (1975)]

There is a wonderful saying 'He who communicates leads'. Or she, as the case may be. I think this is very true. We tend to think of the person who is the most effective at communicating as having leadership qualities and certainly, as a manager, one of the skills that you simply must have is the ability to communicate. The success of your team and the individuals within it will be highly dependent on how well you can communicate and whether you communicate enough of the right kinds of information.

Communication can be broken down into *what* to communicate and *how* to communicate. We also need to consider the manner of the communication, i.e., the words that you choose and the non-verbal aspects of communication.

First I think it useful to establish a definition of communication that we can all apply in the workplace. There are many definitions. The one I propose to work with is:

'Communication is the effective sharing of information that results in understanding and ultimately action.'

The key words are understanding and action. Without understanding there is no action. If you don't understand εφγηι δδιλυψ ξζψπκθ, then I haven't communicated with you. So the key element of communication consists of ensuring that people have understood.

There are two sorts of communication – verbal and non-verbal. And already, just in the use of the word 'verbal' we begin to see how easy it is to miscommunicate. We tend to use the word verbal to apply to the spoken word. However, verbal communication is in fact any kind of communication involving words, so it includes both written and spoken. Non-verbal communication is any kind of communication that doesn't use words. Examples are:

Verbal forms of communication	Non-verbal forms of communciation
● Letters ● Faxes ● Books ● Spoken word ● Newspapers ● Morse code (uses dots and dashes to represent words – therefore is still verbal) ● Semaphore (uses different flags to represent words, therefore is still verbal)	● Body language ● Signs ● Symbols ● Sound ● Music ● Touch ● Expression ● Tone of voice ● Graphs ● Maps ● Pictures ● Eye contact

You can see from the above that even with just a few examples there are more kinds of non-verbal communication than there are verbal.

The skill is to use the best possible combination of communication tools at the best time for a known purpose. There are, however, barriers to communication which need to be overcome. Common barriers include:

- low morale
- stress
- poor environment
- low respect for the person doing the communicating
- heard it before
- de-motivation
- not understanding the message
- not understanding the jargon.

What to communicate

What do people need to know and why do they need to know it? Fundamentally, people need to know things that directly affect their jobs and their ability to carry them out.

- What is my job?
- Who is my boss?
- What contribution does my work make to the overall picture?
- Where does the work come from and go to?
- What are my standards of performance? Why are they set at that level?
- What are my targets?
- How am I doing?
- How are we (the team) doing?
- How are we (the whole organization) doing?
- What are the priorities for my work over the next few months?
- What can I influence?
- What can I do to improve things?

There are many different ways of communicating these kinds of things. I propose to cover the ones you are most likely to get involved in as a manager. You do also need to learn how to write effective reports and letters and make presentations. However, I recommend that you either attend a course or buy a book that specializes in this area. I want to focus on the communication that is going to have most impact on your ability to get your team to deliver the job. This is primarily three forms of communication – one-to-ones, team briefings and managing meetings. All these are face-to-face meetings – which in my view is the most effective way of communicating with people.

Holding effective one-to-ones

A one-to-one (1-1) is one of the most powerful tools you have as a manager if you use it correctly. There are essentially eight characteristics of a 1-1.

1　It is a private, face-to-face meeting between an individual and their line manager (in this case you).
2　The discussion covers the whole job, not just a part of it.
3　It is an informal discussion, but it is nonetheless structured so that it isn't just a 'chat'.
4　It covers the period between the last 1-1 and this one, current work in progress and the future (normally up to the date of the next 1-1 but sometimes further ahead).
5　Notes are kept of actions agreed.
6　The discussion is meant to be two-way in that you, the manager, discuss the performance of the individual and they also get the opportunity to talk about how you are doing as their leader and what could be done to improve the partnership.
7　Each 1-1 will often result in actions being agreed which will be evaluated at the next 1-1.
8　1-1s should allow some time for the individual to chat through how they are feeling generally and how they are getting on with other members of the team.

It is a good idea for you to plan each 1-1 in advance. Keep a 1-1 folder for each individual where you can hold notes, copies of letters, etc. relating to the individual. Then when you come to plan the 1-1 all you will need to do is pull out the file. It means you don't have to try to remember everything. You need to consider the following when planning:

● What where the targets set at the last 1-1 and have they been achieved?
● If not, why not?
● What are the key messages you want to get across?
● What do you want to hear about?
● What have they done that you want to praise them for?

You must *never* use a 1-1 to tell people off or to discipline them. If you need to point out to an individual an action or piece of behaviour that is unacceptable, then do it straight away or arrange a special meeting to talk about it. If you want to invoke the discipline procedure, you need to do it separately from the 1-1. The reason for this is that it is vitally important that people feel 'safe' in their 1-1. If they feel threatened at all, the 1-1 will fall into disrepute and you won't get them to be open and honest with you. 1-1s should be mostly about praise and encouragement.

Roger Moores in his book *Managing for High Performance* gives some simple and effective interviewing tips for 1-1s and a checklist of ten basic skills for 1-1 meetings which I have summarized and adapted here.

- In 1-1s you should talk for approximately 20% of the time and listen for 80%.
- When discussing development, it is best to start with open questions so that you get your team member talking about their feelings about how they are doing.
- Good questions would include:
  - How do you feel your job has been going since we last spoke?
  - What do you feel you do best and what do you feel you could improve?
  - What are your strong points and in what areas of the job do you feel you need development?
  - What problems have you encountered? How did you handle them?
  - What do you like most and least about your job?
  - In what ways could the job be improved?
  - What can I do to help you?
  - What can I do to be a better manager for you?

Ten point checklist for 1-1s

1 Even though you are planning a short discussion, preparation is vital.
2 Have you checked the records (if appropriate) of the team member?
3 Have you checked the facts of the team member's performance such as goals and targets?

4 Have you worked out your main questions?
5 Are they mostly open questions – what, why, when, where, who, how?
6 Have you decided on your interview strategy, i.e., in what order are you going to tackle questions/parts of the job?
7 Have you arranged enough time to discuss everything?
8 Have you arranged the seating so that it is informal and encourages open conversation?
9 Have you got pen and paper so that you can take notes?
10 Have you made sure you will not be disturbed?

A well managed 1-1 will help to motivate the team member, bring any problems out into the open before they turn into major disasters and save hours of monitoring performance.

Team briefing

Hopefully most of you will have a team briefing system in your organization. Team briefing is very simply a method of ensuring systematic and regular communication of issues relevant to organizations and teams.

Most team briefings begin with a cascade. That is, the senior management team get together and decide what core information they want to communicate throughout the organization. It will normally include financial results, positions against targets, changes in policy and priorities for the future. They will brief this to the middle managers, who will in turn brief their first line managers and other direct reports, including in their brief any information which is only relevant to the local team such as changes in work priorities. The first line manager (you) will then usually have the responsibility of communicating the core brief, plus any local information, to their team. The key thing is to make the core brief relevant to your own team, otherwise it just becomes meaningless information. On the whole, 70% of the brief should be about local matters and only 30% core. Even if your organization doesn't have a formal system of briefing, I strongly recommend you introduce your own informal one. You can still more or less keep to the structure I have outlined. To get the 'core' information just ask your manager for it.

You should set aside time to prepare your brief so that it is relevant to the team and you are clear what outcome you want to achieve. Make sure that you allow time for people to ask questions. And, most importantly, if they ask a question to which you don't know the answer, then say something like 'I'm sorry, I don't know the answer to that question, but I'll find out and get back to you'. And then make sure that you do get back to them. It is very easy when briefing to answer a question by speculating. You'll find yourself saying things like 'I expect that's because…' or 'I imagine they think…' and so on. Don't think you won't. It's almost impossible not to. Just look out for it.

Ensure that the team is briefed regularly, at least once every six weeks, preferably once a month.

Managing meetings

'The length of a meeting rises with the square of the number of people present.' [Eileen Shanahan, New York Times Magazine (1968)]

You will find, as a new manager, that you need to start holding meetings with your team and sometimes with other teams. Often you will find yourself having to chair those meetings.

You should try to have a full team meeting where you and the team can talk about plans and priorities for the team. In my first management job I used to hold team meetings every Friday afternoon. We used to spend about an hour planning the work for the following week. We then used to spend half an hour doing 'clear up' where people did filing, sorted out next week's work and so on. Originally, we used to open a bottle of wine and have a glass each and use the time for chatting and for informal team building. But the world has changed since then and there are very few organizations that permit drinking alcohol on the premises during working hours. Of course this is quite right, and I would not tolerate it now. But I must confess, I do rather miss those days. However, the equivalent today would be to have tea and cakes. We all used to look forward to Friday afternoon planning meetings!

People do complain about meetings. However, they are

important. Having everyone in one room for a regular period of time does the following:

● It reinforces the sense that you are all part of one team with one common goal.
● Everyone hears what everyone else has to say so you don't get the 'Chinese whispers' effect.
● People are more likely to offer help and support to each other.
● You can plan the workload more effectively because everyone can share their priorities and difficulties.
● It reinforces your role as the leader.
● It helps team building.
● You can make it fun.

Chairing a meeting is a particular and very important skill. Below is a very simple checklist of things to remember when organizing and chairing meetings.

Before the meeting

● Be clear of the outcome of the meeting. What do you want to achieve and is a meeting the best way of achieving it?
● Prepare your agenda. Even if you are not producing a formal typed agenda make sure that you and the people attending the meeting know what is going to be covered and have the opportunity to prepare.
● Make sure that you allocate a specific start and end time and stick to them.
● Time items on your agenda so that you spend the right amount of time on the important items and don't spend too long on things that are trivial.
● Make sure that any actions agreed at previous meetings have been carried out so you don't waste time at the meeting finding out if people have done things and hearing their excuses for why they haven't.

During the meeting

● Remind everyone of the purpose and objective of the meeting. Check that they know what the agenda is.

- Make sure you sit where you can see and hear everyone.
- Make sure that everyone is comfortable.
- Use a flipchart to make notes of actions so that everyone can see what has been agreed.
- Summarize regularly.
- Stick to the agenda.
- Ensure that every point ends with an agreed action, even if the action is to bring forward to the next meeting.
- Ensure each action has a deadline and the name of the person or people who have committed to carrying it out.
- Keep the meeting fun! A little bit of humour does a lot to make meetings more enjoyable. And if the meeting is enjoyable then it will probably go quicker and be more effective.
- Make sure that everyone who wishes gets the opportunity to speak.

After the meeting

- Make sure that if you are producing minutes they are sent out within about two days. Any longer and people will forget what they were supposed to do.
- Make sure you have fixed the time and date of the next meeting.
- Check that everyone is clear about their actions.
- Chase people's actions before the next meeting is due.
- Communicate any decisions made at the meeting to any people who were unable to attend.

A well run meeting, with clear actions and outcomes, will go a long way towards minimizing the likelihood of things going wrong during the week or month ahead.

Summary and key actions

- Think about what people need to know and why and make that the focus of communication.
- Plan regular 1-1s.
- Make sure your team briefings are relevant to the team.
- Be clear of your objectives and outcomes when you hold meetings.

CHAPTER 8

Managing time, problems and stress

One of the things you will notice very quickly when you become a manager is that you spend much less of your time actually 'producing' things and much more time being productive 'invisibly'. That is, you will spend a fair bit of time talking to people, either formally in 1-1s about their work or informally about their own lives. You will spend time helping them to solve problems and keeping an eye on their motivation and stress levels.

At the same time you will still have to do administrative type tasks, like producing monthly reports or reconciling the monthly figures, or replying to customer complaints, or whatever your particular job entails.

And you are also highly likely to have to spend much more time in meetings!

All of this means that if your old job involved turning up at 9am, or at the beginning of your shift, and then leaving at 5pm, or eight hours later, without taking any work home – you are in for a rude shock. Ask any manager, even the most ruthlessly efficient, and they will tell you that in becoming a manager you are actually signing up for a heavier workload and longer hours. Sometimes, the longer hours are self-inflicted. It's less that the organization requires you to work long hours and more that as a manager you will find that you take such personal responsibility for things that it becomes very difficult to leave jobs undone. In addition, sometimes you will have planned your day only to discover that an unanticipated problem with an individual member of staff takes half a day to sort out.

This is not to put you off, simply to have you recognize that your organization will expect more of you and you will expect more of yourself.

To use your time to the maximum benefit there are three things to be aware of. First, some basic tips on time and workload management. Second, some hints about effective problem solving and, finally, how to look out for and manage stress both in yourself and in your team.

Managing the extra work

Now you have become a manager you will need to be quite ruthless when it comes to prioritizing your work. Essentially you can split your job into the three areas that I talked about in the chapter on leadership. Achieving the task, building the team and developing individuals. Those are the areas that form the overall priorities. Any task that does not fall easily into one of those three headings is probably not that important.

And now, you really do need to distinguish what is important from what is not. An important task is any task that helps you to achieve your overall objective and that of the team.

There are no magic wands for effective time management. There are no filofaxes or systems that if you apply them will change your life. Time management really does boil down to self discipline. And that means, deciding what your priorities are, when you are going to do tasks, and sticking to what you have agreed with yourself.

First you need to make sure that you have a written job description which clearly lays out the core result areas of your job. Second, you need to make sure that each member of your team has the same thing. I would be inclined to call them job summaries rather than descriptions as the word job description does rather smack of inflexibility and 'jobsworth'. Good job summaries should:

● establish a common understanding of the content of the job between the job holder and the manager

- set realistic and agreed job responsibilities, making clear the relationships between jobs to avoid overlapping and gaps
- clarify functions and responsibilities
- clarify levels of authority
- clarify expected outcomes
- provide the job holder with the nature, scope and content of the job
- provide a definition of the organization's expectations of the job holder.

Be sure that you have clearly identified your job objectives and those of your team and also the key result areas, i.e., the parts of the job on which they will be measured.

Example

Overall objective: To manage the research and development team to produce new products for the organization to help maintain and increase income.

Key result areas	Key tasks
1 To organize and plan research and development within the budget limits and to the needs of the organization	
2 To manage and motivate a team of six people to achieve this	● Hold 1-1 meetings each month with every individual ● Hold team briefing meetings on the first Monday of every month ● Carry out annual appraisal with each individual ● Monitor each individual's achievement of his/her objectives and key result areas ● Provide support where necessary ● Report on the team's activities every month
3 To create additional income of [X] during the financial year	
4 To liaise with key customers to try out new products on our behalf	

Reactive and proactive tasks

You are likely to find that much of your day is spent dealing with what we call reactive tasks. Reactive tasks are those jobs that you cannot predict. They are normally jobs which need to be done immediately and interrupt your planned work (proactive tasks).

Most of us, when mentally planning our days, plan to spend almost 100% of the time on proactive tasks. And of course, we live in a world where things go wrong. We get interrupted, things break down, problems occur that need to be sorted out straight away.

That means that we don't get to do all the tasks that we had planned to do, we feel we have failed and we start to fall behind in our work and feel stressed.

Calculate for yourself roughly how much time you think you spend, on average, during a working day on reactive and proactive tasks. And then plan your days accordingly. If seven out of your eight hours tend to be spent in dealing with reactive tasks, then there is no point planning otherwise.

Managing your diary

The diary is a very useful time management tool, particularly for managers.

Most of us tend to underuse the diary. We use it to make appointments to see other people and we tend to keep those commitments. However, we are not so good at keeping commitments to ourselves.

Get into the habit of making appointments in your diary to do tasks. That way, you will know that you have set aside time to do that 'big job' and others will know it too. If for some reason you need to use the time for something else you simply rearrange the appointment, much as you would any other.

Ensure you allow slightly longer for tasks than you think they might take. My experience is that jobs always take at least 20% longer to do in real time than in planned time. If you do finish the job early you've gained extra time!

Example Diary

Time	Monday	Tuesday	Wednesday	Thursday	Friday
0800					
0900	Morning team meeting		1-1 Lesley	Travel to Leeds	Finalize budget
1000		Campaign strategy meeting		Meet Pat in Leeds office	Budget meeting – head office
1100			Work on the budget	Walk the job	
1200	Lunch with Joe				
1300					
1400	1-1 Helen				
1500	Prepare for campaign strategy meeting	Write up notes for monthly report		Travel back to London	Friday planning meeting
1600	1-1 Maria				Admin for next week
1700			Nigel's leaving party		
1800					

Rolling to do lists

A rolling 'to do' list replaces traditional to do lists and time set aside to plan. With a rolling to do list you plan your workload as you go along. You can either use a diary that has a blank facing page or a plain notebook into which you put dates. Then, every time you think of a task that has to be done, or someone asks you to do something and it's too small a task to make an appointment to do, you write in your rolling to do list *on the day on which you intend to do* it. That way you don't have to remember things or write great long lists of things you know you won't get done and that only depress you and send you off to the smoking room or to get a cup of coffee to recover! A rolling to to list might look something like this:

Time	Monday	To do page
0800		
0900	Morning team meeting	● Phone Joe ● Check invoice received from BTB
1000		● Reply to letter from DTI
1100		● Fix up meeting with Patrick –
1200	Lunch with Joe	planning
1300		● Speak to Russ re campaigning
1400	1-1 Helen	column in magazine
1500	Prepare for campaign strategy meeting	● Phone Deborah re Friday night ● Check budget deadline ● Fix 1-1 with Simon
1600	1-1 Maria	
1700		
1800		

If you don't manage to get the job done on the day, you simply rewrite it for the day on which you can do it.

Dealing with paperwork

Somebody told me that the advent of computers meant the paperless office. I sincerely hope that that person didn't go into business on the basis of that comment because I can honestly say that since computers became a regular feature of work (which is not all that long) there has been even more paper landing on my desk. And it sits there in my in-tray, growling occasionally. Eventually, I have to succumb and deal with it. And therein lies the solution to dealing with paperwork. Don't let it sit in your in-tray growling at you, waiting for you to deal with it. The answer is to take some action on every piece of paper that appears on your desk *immediately*. Don't do what we all do, which is flick through it to see what's there. You only end up having to read it twice which really is a waste of time.

Set aside a regular time each day to deal with your post and either action immediately (e.g., write the reply to the letter/ memo, make the phone call), put it into the bring forward to be dealt with later (I'll cover next how a bring forward works), or put it into the bin. Do *not* use a pending tray. Pending trays breed profusely. They multiply pieces of paper.

The bring forward system

A bring forward system is a concertina file or drawer full of lateral files, that is numbered 1 to 31 and has sections for the months. You simply put your piece of paper into the slot of the day on which you want it taken out to reappear on your desk to be dealt with. Things that would go in there would be agendas for meetings, copies of letters that you want to check you've had a response to, notes to remind yourself to do things and so on. I put bills in there to remind me to pay them too, plus birthday cards ready for people's birthdays.

Problem solving

Solving problems takes on an added dimension of challenge when you are a manager, because one of the key things you have to try to do is not to solve other people's problems for them, but help them to solve their own.

Also, if you have delegated a task to someone you need to make sure that you also allow them the freedom to fix their own errors.

Problem solving is linked to decision taking because it is through taking the right decisions that you will solve the problem.

Decision taking can be quite nerve-racking. You might worry about what others think, or try to please other people. When you are a new manager it is possible that you are unsure about the limits of your authority. Sometimes, you may not even recognize that there is a problem that needs to be solved. The thing to remember is that there is no perfect decision. Fundamentally a decision is simply a choice of taking a particular action rather than another or sometimes taking no action at all. There is no magical 'right' decision which it is your job to find.

You don't find the right answer, you simply make informed choices and then try to make them work. And if they don't work, you make a new choice based on a new set of information. If you think about it like that, it should help to take some of the anxiety out of decisions.

There are four simple stages to problem solving – analyze, choose, implement and evaluate.

Identify and analyze the problem

First you need to be sure that you are dealing with the problem and not simply the symptom. An analogy is that of having recurring headaches. You could go to the doctor who would give you aspirin for it. But the real problem may be that you are allergic to chocolate and that in order to solve the headache problem you need to stop eating chocolate. Another example may be that a member of your team made a mistake when they produced some figures for you. On the surface it may look as if they added the figures up wrong. On the other hand, it might be that they actually don't understand how to produce the figures because they didn't have any training. And that's the problem that you need to tackle.

Differentiate between a crisis and a problem. It is very easy to either over- or under-estimate the severity of a problem. Answer the following questions:

● What exactly is the problem?
● When does it need to be sorted out by?
● Who is involved?
● What are the consequences if I don't deal with it?
● What will be the result if it gets solved?
● Who can help?
● What is the outcome that I am looking for?
● Why did it happen?

Identify and choose options

You now need to consider all the alternative choices that you have. To generate choices, this is the stage at which you might consult others and seek their views and opinions. What do they think is a solution? Don't over-consult, you don't always need to seek people's agreement in order to make a decision. Ask yourself the following questions:

● How many choices do I have?
● Do I have to take the decision now?
● Do I have to take a decision at all?
● What are the pros and cons of each possible option?
● What do others think?

Sometimes there is no obvious 'best' decision. There are times when you have to choose the least worst option.

Implement

Having made your decision you now need to communicate it. Even if you feel unsure, you need to communicate it with confidence. However, be prepared to change your mind if new information comes to light or if it becomes obvious that there is another, better option. Do remember that you must explain why you have chosen the option that you have. That doesn't mean be apologetic or justify. It means having people understand on what basis you made your decision.

Ask yourself the following questions:

● Who needs to know about this decision?
● Who has to implement it?
● Have I given them all the information they need?
● Have I explained the reason for this decision?
● Have I recorded my action anywhere?
● How will I monitor the implementation of the decision?

Evaluate

This is one of the most important parts of problem solving and decision taking and is the one most often left out. You need to ask yourself:

● Was the problem solved?
● Did a better option appear?
● Was the decision implemented?
● What could be done to avoid the same problem occurring again?

Helping others to solve their own problems

One of the key attributes of a good manager is that they don't
solve other people's problems for them. There are very good
reasons for this. If you solve other people's problems for them
they will never learn how to solve them for themselves. In
addition, it will add to your workload. As a manager your role
is to help others solve their own problems, not to do it for them.

There are a number of actions that you can take which will
encourage them to solve their own problems while at the same
time not looking as if you are not being helpful.

- Ask open questions – 'What options do you have?'
- Use 'we' language if appropriate. Say things like, 'What can
  we do about it?'
- Or use 'you' language – 'What do you think you ought to do?'
- Get them to think through using the same process as I gave
  you earlier, i.e., analyze, choose, implement and evaluate.

Never tell people they made a wrong decision. If they didn't
solve the problem, or if the action they took didn't work then
what you need to do is help them analyze why and then make a
new choice which will produce the result they want.

Above all, don't try and manipulate them into making the
decision you want them to make. And if you don't agree with the
decision they take you must still support it. Just as you would
expect your manager to support your decisions. And finally, never
overturn their decisions. Talk them into overturning it themselves
if they need to. You need to try to maintain their confidence.

Identifying and managing other people's stress

Part of your job as a manager is to be aware of the stress levels
in other people. You need to be able to recognize the symptoms
and take action where appropriate.

Stress in itself is not a bad thing. We all need a certain level
of stress in order to operate at our optimum. Too little stress is
as bad for us as too much. The other thing about stress is that it
is a very individual thing. Dr John Edmondson, a practising

psychologist specializing in stress, uses the analogy of a lion suddenly entering the room. Most of us would get a stress reaction because we are afraid and can't deal with the lion. However, one of you might be secretly practising to be a lion tamer and feel a very positive stress response because you think you have the tools to deal with this lion.

So, what is hugely stressful for one person may be an exciting challenge for somebody else. As a manager you need to look out for signs of stress that are unhealthy and take action. Signs to look out for are:

- Is the person suffering from lots of headaches and general maladies?
- Do they seem to be overtired?
- Are they bad or short tempered?
- Are they smoking or drinking excessively?
- Do they seem unable to cope with small or trivial problems?
- Do they over react to things going wrong?
- Do they exhibit a lot of frustration?
- Are they generally snapping at people?
- Do they have problems concentrating?
- Do they appear to be disorganized?
- Do they appear to have changed in character (i.e., if they were bubbly have they become quiet? If they were quiet have they become loud?).

These are just some examples. There are no prescriptive symptoms.

If you have identified what appears to be a problem with stress in a team member, the first thing to do is to talk to them about it. But make sure that you are being seen to be being supportive and not accusing them of being unable to cope. People who are suffering from excess stress will often be reluctant to admit to it because they don't want you to think that they are unable to cope. If they won't talk to you, suggest someone else.

You might ask them questions like:

- On the whole are you happy in your job?
- Do you have the right tools/materials to do your job?
- Do you have a good working relationship with me? With the rest of the team?

- Is your working environment right for what you do?
- Are you spending too much time at work, or working at home?
- Are you spending time worrying about work?
- Do you have enough leisure time?
- Do you spend enough time on yourself?
- Do you need time off?
- What can I do to help?

Getting the balance right between support and stress

This is a particularly important area which often gets neglected. Too much stress is bad for people. Too little stress is bad for people. Enough stress and you get high performance. John Edmondson showed me the following model.

Managing stress model

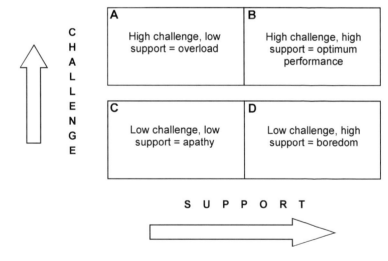

We all operate out of these quadrants at different times. For example, sometimes when the pressure is on at work you won't have enough time to provide support to your team because the job needs to be done. This is fine in the short term, but eventually you need to pull back and give them some more support. Sometimes people need lots of support but little challenge, for example, if thcy have a personal problem, so they will be in quadrant D. Sometimes, people just need to be left alone for a bit in which case they will be in quadrant C. Mostly, however, the ideal place for your team to operate is out of quadrant B, high challenge and high support. This is part of your job as the manager.

Some things to think about to achieve this:

● Have you asked your team recently if they feel they have enough challenge?
● Have you asked them if they feel supported?
● Do you know what's going on in their lives? (Not necessarily the intimate details, but you do need to have a general idea.)
● Are you ensuring that any tasks they are being set are achievable, even if the task is challenging?
● Does your team feel they can approach you with problems, either personal ones or work-related ones?
● Do you monitor absenteeism to check that people aren't staying off work because they can't cope?

At the end of the day, people will need to sort out their own stress. However, you can be vigilant. Mostly, however, just showing people that you care about them can be of the biggest support.

Summary and key actions

● Plan for things to go wrong.
● Make sure you are solving the problem not the symptom.
● Get the balance right between support and stress.
● Use your diary to plan your work.
● Make yourself available to your team to share their problems.

CHAPTER 9

Your responsibility for health and safety

'*Life's not just being alive, but being well.*' [Martial]

It is very easy to imagine that, simply because you might work in an office and not on a factory floor, health and safety is not an issue that needs to concern you. However, in the UK this is absolutely not the case. Quite apart from what makes good management sense, health and safety legislation in the UK has become more sophisticated and affects more areas of work and more levels of management. Even if it is not specified in your contract of employment, managers are required to implement policies and comply with legislation whatever the subject. And as many of you know, ignorance of the law is not a defence.

Health and safety law aims to reduce accidents and ill health caused by or at work. It is certainly true that the balance of work in the UK has moved from a traditional manufacturing base to a service base and therefore office or shop based. You might think, therefore, that health and safety is less of an issue. However, there is still a very high rate of accidents and ill health recorded in the workplace. Approximately 500 people in the UK die each year in work-related incidents. 500 people is too many. There are probably at least three times as many incidents that occur in the workplace than are reported.

In addition, there are more issues included under health and safety law than there were before. For example, violence, bullying, harassment, excess working hours, stress and so on. UK law has changed to reflect the fact that employers are required not simply to provide a safe place for people to work, but also that they support individuals who may be affected by an adverse work environment.

I don't propose to go into detail about the law in the UK. This is not a comprehensive listing, and more specific advice should be sought from your HR manager. This book will highlight some key duties and responsibilities and some basic actions you can take to ensure that you are providing a safe and healthy environment.

The key tasks of management

Under the Management of Health and Safety at Work Regulations 1992, there are a number of key tasks. This chapter aims to give you a basic understanding of what some of the ones that affect you as a UK manager involve. The Health and Safety Executive offer the following advice to organizations to comply with regulation 4 'To establish procedures for the effective planning, organization, control, monitoring and review of health and safety'.

Policy

You need to ensure that your organization has a health and safety policy and that you know and understand what it contains and how it affects you, your team and your work environment. The policy is likely to include information about how the organization ensures that there is no health and safety risk to customers or visitors to the premises. If you haven't seen one, you must ask for it. You must read it. And most importantly of all, you must make sure that your team have read and understood it. And as manager you must ensure that you comply with the policy.

Define responsibilities

Your organization should clearly define who is responsible for which aspect of its health and safety policy. You should be told in your induction what your specific duties and responsibilities are. If you weren't told you need to find out. Your team should also be aware of what role they play in making the health and safety policy work. You also need to be sure that you know who the health and safety representatives are and what their roles are. It is important that you understand that the responsibility for health and safety within an organization is not the job of only the health and safety representatives. Their job is to help monitor and support management in applying the policy and complying with the law. You are part of that management now.

Standards

Most organizations will set down standards for health and safety policy implementation. The standards are likely to include things that directly relate to health and safety as well as whatever procedures might apply where there has been a breach of policy or legislation. The organization may have standards for absenteeism, sickness, and accidents to be monitored and reduced or contained. In addition, there may be standards that you are expected to apply as a manager. Certainly, you will need to set and monitor standards within your team such as moving boxes out of corridors, not using fire extinguishers to prop open fire doors, keeping corridors and entrance ways clear and so on.

Monitor

The organization will have some method of monitoring compliance with policy and legislation. This is often where health and safety representatives come in. However, you have a duty as a manager to report anything that is likely to constitute a risk to health and safety. If you cannot fix the problem yourself, you must report it to someone who can. If you knowingly ignore a situation which is potentially a risk to the health and safety of your team you may be held liable for any subsequent accidents or ill health occurring as a result. This includes such small and obvious things as boxes in corridors.

Audit

Organizations should also do a regular audit. If yours doesn't appear to, you should ask for it.

Training

There are specific duties in the UK for training in health and safety and European law is giving more attention to this area. Training has to be provided for people who are clearly at risk, who work with potentially dangerous equipment or who need instructions to operate new machinery or equipment.

Whatever the legislation, there are sensible things that you can do as a manager to ensure that people really understand.

You must make sure that new employees are trained in health and safety generally and, where appropriate, on the use of equipment and machinery as soon as is practically possible after joining, and most certainly before they are exposed to something potentially hazardous.

You should also ensure that your team understand how to recognize potential danger and what action they should take when they do so.

Incidentally, you should also provide an adequate level of instruction for temporary or sub-contracted staff.

When allocating tasks to an individual you have a duty to also take into account their 'capabilities as regards health and safety', whether they are a new or existing employee. You are also required to recognize and allow for physical or psychological disabilities. The Disability Discrimination Act 1995 specifically provides for individuals with disabilities to be enabled by employers to carry out tasks. This means that the employer, where practicable and reasonable, will be expected to adjust the working environment to accommodate them.

Risk assessments

Much of the UK legislation around health and safety requires that risk assessments are carried out. Essentially, a risk assessment is simply a procedure to analyze the potential hazard of a situation and what can be done to contain it. Very often risk assessments are carried out by line managers, which is you. Incidentally, a side benefit is that this is an excellent way of finding out how people do their jobs, arrange their work stations and so on.

There is an approved code of practice (ACOP) for carrying

out risk assessments. In his book *Risk Assessment*, Pat McGuinness writes about the five steps to risk assessment recommended by the Health and Safety Executive. They are:

1 Look for hazards.
2 Decide who might be harmed and how.
3 Evaluate the risks arising from the hazards and decide whether the existing precautions are adequate or require further action.
4 Record your findings.
5 Review your assessment from time to time and amend if necessary.

Checklist of actions you can take to have a healthy working environment

- Make sure that you lead by example. People will only take health and safety seriously if you are seen to do so also.
- Find out how to identify a potential hazard. I strongly recommend that you ask your organization for some health and safety traning.
- If you see a potential hazard (and remember a hazard might not involve machinery, it may simply be a fire door left open or an overloaded filing cabinet) then you must remedy it or report it and be seen to do so.
- If you see someone taking an action which is potentially hazardous you must tell them about it, even if they don't report to you directly.
- If someone breaks the health and safety policy persistently then you must take appropriate action. This may sometimes involve the discipline procedure.
- Ensure that you have fully communicated to new members of your team the health and safety policy and how it applies to them.
- Where your team are heavy users of VDUs make sure that they take regular eye tests and that a risk assessment has been carried out on their work station.
- Know where the accident book is kept and how to use it.
- Monitor and correct potentially dangerous practices such as using unauthorized appliances (kettles, fans, sandwich makers), insecure equipment, blocked passageways.

- Make sure people aren't overloading electrical sockets.
- Take action to ensure that wires aren't trailing across the floor.
- Find out what legislation applies to the work done by your team and get to know it in more detail.
- If you have asked for a safety improvement to be made, follow it up until you are sure it has been carried out.

Remember, health and safety is only expensive when employers get it wrong and find themselves faced with large fines or, worse still, serious damage to the health of an employee.

Summary and key actions

- Know your responsibilities.
- Communicate responsibilities for health and safety to your team.
- Don't ignore potentially hazardous situations.
- Carry out risk assessments where required and regularly.
- Monitor.

CHAPTER 10

Performance management – getting the best out of your team

Performance management sounds grand, doesn't it? And yet you needn't be intimidated by it. Actually, a lot of what you need to do to manage performance we have already talked about, because essentially a manager's job is to manage performance. However, most organizations will have some specific performance management systems (also known as appraisal systems) which they will expect you to implement.

Performance management means making sure that the objectives and aims of the individuals in your team match the needs of the organization, that individuals are meeting or exceeding standards and targets and that there is a method for helping them to improve when they fall behind, which most people will do at some point.

Good performance management, whatever the specifics of your system, covers what people need to know:

- What is my job?
- Who is my boss?
- What am I measured on?
- How am I doing?
- What do I need to do next?

Job summary (job description)

Every member of your team should have a job summary which lays out their key result areas (those areas of work on which they will be measured) and standards set against each area, what their key responsibilities are, what their levels of responsibility are, who they report to and how they will be measured.

Even if *you* don't have an accurate or up to date job summary that is not an excuse for your team not to have one.

Generally speaking, unless you are designing a brand new job it is better for the individual to write the job summary which is then agreed by you. A simple layout for a job summary might look something like this:

Key result area	Key tasks	Standards of performance
Administration	Dealing with correspondence	● Open post by 0930 am daily ● Reply to letters within 24 hours
	Filing of documents	● File documents according to file system ● Filing tray to be empty at least weekly
Financial figures	Processing invoices	● Process invoices within 48 hours ● Copy all paid invoices to the manager
	Reconciling monthly accounting report	● Add up the total of all invoices weekly ● Accrue for invoices not received monthly ● Produce report by the first Monday of the month

You will note that I have used the terms Key Tasks and Standards of Performance. A key task is a key result area broken down into a smaller component, in other words the specific thing that needs to be done in order to achieve the key result area.

Standards of performance

People are often confused about what a standard of performance is and what it relates to. A standard of performance or SOP is a statement of the minimum requirement the organization has for that particular job or task. SOPs always apply to the job and not to the individual, although clearly there will be instances where individuals do not meet the standard for whatever reason, for example they may be new.

It is important that all jobs have standards because you need to ensure a consistency of delivery of a product or service. For example, if a company that made baked beans did not ensure that all baked beans tins weighed the same then they would soon find themselves losing customers. Or if a customer found that they kept being charged a different price for the same goods, or that different kinds of house style came out of the same organization, they would begin to doubt how good or reliable the organization was and eventually you would probably lose their business.

It is important that SOPs are written down and agreed so that both you and your team have a good understanding of what is required. It also makes it easier for you to measure and monitor. If the standard is clear, you often don't need to point out when the standard is falling because the team member will be aware of it themselves.

Standards of performance can contain the following characteristics:

Quantity: e.g., measurement of numbers of sales achieved, customers served, shoes sold, etc.
Timed: e.g., meeting of deadlines, turnaround of correspondence, speed of dealing with complaints, etc.
Financial: e.g., amount of sales, cost of expenditure, price of goods bought, delivery to budget, etc.
Quality: e.g., level to which a job is carried out, the 'appearance' of a document, the way in which the telephone is answered, etc.

Targets

There are many reasons to set targets. For example:

- to develop individuals and progressively train them
- to change priorities where circumstances dictate it
- to encourage continuous improvement of performance
- to re-establish slipping targets (or standards)
- to promote innovation
- to broaden skills
- to develop new areas of work
- to achieve things that otherwise get neglected
- to focus attention on priorities
- to assist work planning
- to improve job satisfaction.

There are three kinds of targets – training, developmental and remedial.

Training targets

A training target is a target that you give to an individual who is new to a job or task and who cannot be expected to achieve the standard of performance immediately. The training target will contain a number of small steps to help them to achieve their targets.

Developmental targets

A developmental target is one you give to an individual who is consistently meeting the standard and where you want to raise the standard or where you want to set them a different kind of standard to develop their skills.

Remedial targets

A remedial target is one where an individual has fallen below the standard of performance and you want to bring them back up to standard. A simple diagram (opposite) expresses these three kinds of targets:

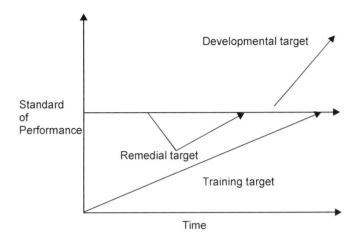

When you set your targets – whether they are for individuals or for teams – you need to follow the SMARTER principle.

S Specific – clear and easy to understand.
M Measurable – so that people will know when they've been achieved.
A Achievable – so that they are possible to achieve.
R Realistic – so they don't overstretch or become meaningless.
T Timed – with an agreed deadline for achieving them.
E Evaluated – how well were they achieved?
R Reviewed – what do the next set of targets need to be?

Most of all you need to ensure that you *agree* targets with your team. If the target is not agreed then it will not be delivered. Don't make the same mistake I did, that I told you about in my introduction, of setting targets for the sake of it. Don't set the target if it isn't going to directly benefit the business or the individual's development of either themselves or the job.

Performance review

Performance review is the process by which you discuss with individuals in your team how they have performed against the standards required of them and the targets that they have been set.

In Chapter 7 I talked about 1-1s. If you are having them regularly then you are actually carrying out a mini-performance review.

A yearly performance review or appraisal is simply a more formal version of the 1-1s that you have had during the year. You talk for about 20% of the time about this year's performance and about 80% of the time about the standards, targets and objectives for next year's performance.

You need to check out your own organization's performance review system. Do ask for training in how to run an appraisal or performance review interview. However, regardless of the system there are a number of things that you can do to make sure the review is effective.

Before

- Keep a note of 1-1s during the year and copies of information, thank you letters, etc., about the individual.
- Have a pre-review meeting where you and the individual agree what areas the review is going to cover and what preparation you are both going to do.
- Encourage the individual to seek the views of the people they work with directly in the team and perhaps some customers or suppliers.
- Agree who you will talk to and who they should talk to.
- Check on the performance against standards.
- Work out the main areas you want to cover and what questions you are going to ask.

During the review

- Allow enough time (I would recommend at least one and a half hours) and make sure you will not be disturbed.
- Remember, let the individual do most of the talking – it is their review.
- Review their key result areas and targets.
- Get them to tell you how they think they have done during the review period (which will normally be a year) – you will find that often people are well aware of what they do well and what they do less well. It is much better to let them identify it than for you to tell them.

● There should be no surprises. Essentially, this should be an opportunity for you to praise and motivate individuals. If performance has been poor, it should have been identified during the year.

● Spend the greater part of the discussion focusing on what they need to do for the coming year. There isn't much you can do about what's already happened apart from praise and reward or work out remedial targets. Much better to concentrate on things they can affect in the future.

● Set new SMARTER targets for the coming year.

● Make sure that both you and the individual take notes.

● Praise as often as you reasonably can. This is often the only chance they get to hear lots of concentrated good stuff about themselves. Don't stint on it, but remember the four Rs of praise I talked about in Chapter 6.

● Make sure you spend time talking about training and development needs for the next year. At the end of the review you need to have agreed a development plan.

After

● At The Industrial Society we encourage staff to write up their own performance reviews and they are then read and agreed by the line manager. This shows that we trust them and also, because we had a discussion and agreed what we both thought about the performance during the review, there will be no surprises in what they write. However, your organization may operate differently. I must say, I do prefer our method – having the line manager write up your appraisal smacks a bit of school reports to me.

● Produce the paperwork quickly. The longer you leave it, the less likely it will be done.

● Write up the development plan and begin action immediately where you can.

Managing poor performance

It is actually quite easy to manage people who consistently do well. But what do you do if someone is simply not performing well at all? First, put it into perspective, most people do well enough most of the time. Second, make sure that you are not unfairly comparing their performance with the 'star' in the team.

Remember also that if they are not performing well it does not necessarily mean that they are rubbish at their job. There may be any number of reasons and you need to think through the possibilities before you start disciplining people.

Possible reasons might be:

- They feel de-motivated.
- The standards or targets set are too high.
- They need more training to do the job.
- There is a problem within the team.
- They have a personal problem which is affecting their performance at work.
- They are in the wrong job.

Most of all you need to be sure that *you* are not the problem. Are you managing them properly? Are you treating them as fairly and equally as you do others? Do you like them and if you don't is that affecting your treatment of them? You need to be really honest with yourself. We are all human and it may be that you are the one at fault.

Whatever the reason you need to have a conversation with the individual to establish what the gaps in performance are, what the reasons for those gaps might be and what action you can take to remedy them.

You need to give people an opportunity to improve on performance so once you have identified the gaps you need to agree what training might be needed and what the deadlines are for improvement. If you believe it is a disciplinary matter then you need to refer to your organization's discipline and grievance procedure to make sure that you implement it correctly.

Whatever else, remember that good managers don't aim to get rid of people. They aim to get people to deliver the job to the standard required and to higher levels of performance where appropriate. The aim of the discipline procedure is not to sack people, but to help people, in a systematic way, to do a good job.

Summary and key actions

- Make sure your team have a job summary that is up to date and regularly reviewed.
- Be sure that standards of performance are written down and understood.
- Set targets that will benefit both the individual and the organization.
- When managing poor performance look to your management of the person first.
- Allow your staff to write up their own review paperwork.

CHAPTER 11

Understanding the money

'Money…is none of the wheels of trade: it is the oil which renders the motion of the wheels more smooth and easy.' [David Hume (1741)]

As a manager you are now likely, perhaps for the very first time, to be expected to have some understanding of accounting procedures and practices in your organization. It is also entirely possible that you are actually responsible for administering a budget, either sales or expenditure, or both. If you are not used to figures you may feel somewhat intimidated by the thought of having to understand company accounts.

However, finance is fairly straightforward if you simply ignore the jargon and concentrate only on what you need to know. If you can manage and understand your own money – budgeting, saving, paying bills and buying things – then you can understand company figures, because essentially they operate on the same principles. I'm not going to go into any detail, nor am I going to explain every aspect. I am going to define some basic terms so that you have an understanding of what they are and talk in a little more detail about those things that might directly affect you. However, if your job is likely to involve you in more regular figure work, I suggest you get some training.

Profit and loss accounts

All organizations have to produce a profit and loss account. (Non-profit making organizations will call it the income and expenditure account). The profit and loss account describes what the income has been for the year, what the expenditure has been, what interest has been earned or paid, what money is owed to it and what money it owes that has been put aside, how much tax it pays and, finally, how much profit has been made. It is essentially a summary of the financial performance of the period.

All businesses need to operate at a certain level of 'profit', because they need to set aside money either to pay shareholders or to re-invest in the organization. This means that their income needs to exceed their expenditure. Occasionally it is enough just to break even, in other words to have no surplus of income over expenditure. However, this is not usually sustainable as most organizations will need to re-invest in new equipment or properties or may want to hire more staff and so will need extra money.

Non-profit organizations such as charities and voluntary bodies will at the very least want to break even and many want to make a surplus to set money aside for a rainy day or to re-invest.

'Annual income twenty pounds, annual expenditure nineteen pounds, nineteen shillings and sixpence, result happiness. Annual expenditure twenty pounds nought and sixpence, result misery.' [Mr Micawber, *David Copperfield*, Charles Dickens]

Balance sheets

A balance sheet is a snapshot of the business at a given point in time and describes the assets owned by the organization, the money it is owed (debtors) and money it owes (creditors).

Fixed assets and depreciation

Sometimes an organization may need to buy something that it won't use up quickly. It may buy a fixed asset which it needs for running its business (e.g., equipment, buildings, machinery) where it needs to spread the cost over a period of time. This is called a fixed asset and essentially depreciation means spreading the cost of such a purchase over a period of time, normally its useful lifetime.

Cash flow

Cash flow is the money that flows in and out of an organization's bank account. Organizations need cash in the bank to pay bills and salaries, just as we need cash to pay our mortgages and so on. Cash flow needs to be monitored closely to ensure that there is enough money in the bank at the right time to pay for things like salaries, etc. Managing cash flow, particularly in large organizations, can be a big job. Because of things being bought and depreciated, the cash flow is different from the profit.

An organization needs to be viable. Viability simply means that the organization is financially able to sustain itself. An organization can be profitable but not viable because it has no cash. It can also be viable but not profitable because there is cash now but it is going to run out.

Sometimes there will be a lot of cash in the bank because invoices haven't yet been paid, but the organization will be in trouble because overall it is not running profitably. It has a lot of cash at the moment, but this will run out because it is not making enough money from selling its products or services.

Turnover

This is the term used to describe the total value of all sales, including those sales that have been invoiced but the cash hasn't yet been received.

Working capital

This is the term used to describe cash that is either held as stock (e.g., the 'raw' material that your organization uses to produce things), or money that is owed to you by others. Basically, you don't want to tie up your cash in working capital that isn't being used because that means you can't use the money for something else. As a manager, you have some control over this in what you choose to spend money on and how much stock you keep. On a balance sheet working capital is often termed 'current assets'.

Net current assets also include creditors, i.e., those people to whom we owe money. Most organizations do not pay their creditors immediately and therefore some of their working capital is in effect funded by the creditors.

Accruals

As a manager you need to understand accruals. When you accrue for something you are making an allowance to pay for something where you have already used the service or product, but haven't yet had the invoice. It's a bit like putting money aside to pay your credit card bill. You've already bought the goods, but you haven't yet had to pay for them. You need to accrue in order that your monthly accounts reflect the real value that you have spent in the month, even though you may not have actually forked out the cash yet. If you don't accrue, when the invoice does come in it will show up in a month when you didn't actually incur the cost. This will affect the look of the figures and may result in people making the wrong decisions about how much money to allow for things in the next year's budget. If you consistently forget to accrue, your year end position may end up being worse than you predicted.

Forecasts

Most organizations produce forecasts. A forecast is simply an estimate of what your income and expenditure is going to be in future months compared to your budget, so that you can make decisions about actions you may need to take. Forecasts are *very important* because if you can see that you are going to have some difficult times ahead, you may choose not to spend money on something or have to make some economies.

Variances

A variance is the difference between what you planned and what actually happened. For example, if you budgeted to have an income of £20,000 and you only produced £15,000 you have negative variance of £5,000. If you produced £22,000 you have a positive variance of £2,000.

Budgeting

Most managers find themselves having to either produce a budget or contribute to the production of one.

A budget is basically the organization's plans for the next financial year expressed in financial terms. Each small part of the budget is meant to contribute to this overall budget – the overall plan.

Normally your organization will lay out in its budget papers what kind of growth it is looking for and what the parameters are that you can work around. You need to make sure you know what the organization expects.

Anthony Greenall in *Finance and Budgeting for Line Managers* describes seven simple steps to successful budgeting.

1 Define your objectives

● What specific things do you want to achieve next year?
● What plans do you have to improve or maintain performance?
● What resources will be needed to deliver the objectives, current and additional?
● What kind of growth does the organization want to see?

2 Define responsibility

● What additional responsibilities might you have next year?
● What are the limits of your authority? What can you make provision for this year yourself and what do you need to seek permission for?
● What responsibilities might you lose this year which affect your budget?

3 Gather the facts

● Be systematic about applying your common sense.
● Collect information on variances on the current budget to date.

- Find out what adjustments the organization wants you to make to cover for inflation and any other costs such as allowances for salary increases.
- Plan time to do preliminary calculations which can be checked.
- Consult and talk to other budget holders and other people who may impact on your budget or on whose budget you might impact.

4　Decide what to submit

- Keep a note of the reasons for your decisions even when they are based on 'hunches' or your gut instinct. This is often called an 'audit trail'. Don't be fooled – even the most carefully researched budget is at best a 'guess' of what may happen in the future.
- Use your common sense and judgement. If something doesn't 'feel' quite right then rethink it.
- Think about what contingencies you might build into your budget to cope with unpredictability.

5　Test and check

- Double check that you have allowed for the differences in month lengths and made adjustments for bank holidays, etc.
- Allow for your work patterns, seasonal adjustments to buying patterns, etc.
- Don't worry too much if you can't always accurately predict when any expenditure or income will fall. Sometimes your best guess has to be good enough. Sometimes it is better to spread the money evenly over associated months.
- Check that it adds up – even if you are using a spreadsheet.
- Does it meet the needs of the business? Will it help you to deliver your departmental objectives for the next year?

6　Win approval

- Make sure that the budget is laid out in a way that is consistent with the requirements of your organization.
- Ensure that where fuller explanation is needed it is easy to go from the financial figure to the fuller explanation.

● Write an overall summary which explains your objectives for the coming year and points to any areas of particular interest or where there is a significant negative or positive change which needs fuller explanation.

● Remember that most people have to re-do their budgets several times because the finance department/director need to reconcile everyone's budgets in the organization to meet the whole. Don't be surprised if you need to re-do or make substantial amendments. This is quite common although tedious and time-consuming.

● Communicate the key components of your budget to your staff. Remember, once it gets approved they are the ones who have to implement it.

● If you have to change it keep notes of what you have changed and why – you never know, you may need to change it back again or refer to your original submission at some point in the future.

7 Live with the budget

● No matter how carefully you have put your budget together, the future is not predictable. The budget is only a map by which you can decide where you want to be and see where you have reached.

● Your job now is to keep an eye on how you are performing against budget. With it you will be comparing your actual performance against your budget because that is what will tell you how well you are doing.

● You are likely to find that you have variances against budget each month. Provided that the variance is not too great and is more or less what you anticipate there isn't a problem. However, often people think that to massively underspend, for example, is a good thing. However, if the variance is regularly too great, whether it's negative or positive, it means that there may be something wrong with your budget.

● Make sure that you are sufficiently informed about your performance against budget so that you can identify any significant problems before they occur and remedial action can be taken.

Remember that many important decisions in organizations are taken on the basis of current and forecast performance against budget. Always be sure you are well informed and have investigated any significant variances.

Above all, get into a good, friendly supportive relationship with your accounts department. They will always be able to help if you get into difficulties.

Summary and key actions

- Find out your specific financial responsibilities.
- Do what you can to make sure that you don't hoard unnecessary stock, therefore tying up capital.
- Keep accruals up to date.
- When planning your budget use your common sense.
- Remember that once your budget is agreed, communicate it to your team – you can't achieve it without their understanding and co-operation.

CHAPTER 12

Recruitment and selection

Now that you have become a manager it is likely that at some point you will have to recruit a new member of your team. Recruitment and selection are at best an inexact science and if you are new to it it can be very daunting.

Recruiting people is an expensive business, which is why it is important that you should try to get it as right as possible. For a start, if you use a recruitment agency you will have to pay a fee to them for recruiting someone that they recommended, and they're not cheap! If you decide to do your own recruitment, you will normally have to pay for the cost of advertising the position. And if no-one suitable applies you have to pay the cost of re-advertising.

Then, once you have selected someone, you have to bear the cost of training the new person to the standard you need for the job. Very few people are able simply to walk straight into a new job and perform at the level required immediately. Most people take some time to settle in.

If the person you selected was wrong for the job and doesn't stay then you have to start the whole process all over again. Very tedious and very expensive!

And finally, if you appointed someone internally and it turns out the job is not right for them, you risk losing a good member of the organization because they are in the wrong job and there isn't another one for them.

In reality, there is no magic formula which you can apply to guarantee that you get the right person for the job. The most you can do is attempt to be as objective and focused as possible about the requirements of the job and the best kind of person to fulfil them.

You also need to be aware of your responsibilities towards equal opportunities and non-discrimination in your method of recruitment.

Equal opportunities and discrimination

We are all prejudiced or biased to a greater or lesser degree. Quite apart from any moral considerations, or the legislation in the UK designed to prevent discrimination on the basis of illogical prejudice, it actually makes very poor business sense to be influenced by prejudice when you are recruiting to fill a position. You need to choose the person who is going to be the best for the job.   Nor do you want to recruit someone towards whom you feel biased because, although you may like them, it's entirely possible that they are not the right person for the job.

So how do you ensure that your selection procedure ensures objectivity as far as possible and avoids discrimination and bias in your selection decisions?

Preparing to recruit – job specifications and person profiles

Before you either approach an agency or advertise externally or internally you need to write up the job specification. The job spec (as it is called) is basically the job summary with rather more detail than normal. The job spec will help to identify what kind of job it is and will separate out the requirements of the job from the previous job holder. It is very tempting as a manager either to recruit the clone of the previous job holder if they were good or the exact opposite if they weren't! Re-writing the job spec will help to remind you of what is needed by the business/organization.

Answer the following questions:

- What is the job title? (Make sure that it reflects the job and not the gender or race of the job-holder. For example, manageress, waitress, odd-job man, post boy, girl Friday, etc.).
- Where is the job to be located in the country and where situated in the building?
- Who will the job holder report to?
- What is the overall purpose of the job?
- What are the levels of authority in the job?
- What are the key result areas?
- Who will the job holder be required to work with?
- What are the terms and conditions of the job?
- What are the career prospects, if any, of the job?

Person profiles

Having identified the key elements of the job you are now in a better position to establish what kind of person you need to fill it.

I want to make some basic points here. The personal circumstances of an individual are not relevant to their ability to do a job. The fact that they live near or far away is not relevant to their ability to do the job. The fact that a person is single, just married or getting divorced; or has children under or over ten, or no children; or is male or female; or black or white; or young or old; or from an ethnic minority; or lives on a council estate; or went to public school or comprehensive school; or is green with purple spots – *is not relevant to their ability to do the job* (except in very specific cases). This includes, for example, lifting and carrying. One might assume that men are stronger than women, and perhaps many are. But not all, and therefore it is not reasonable (or lawful in the UK) to exclude a woman from a lifting job simply because she is a woman and therefore may not be stronger than a man. What you can do is specify the kinds of weights that have to be lifted, but if a woman applies and is able to lift them then you cannot exclude her from the possibility of the job.

You must not, therefore, prepare a person profile which is worded in such a way that you discriminate indirectly. You can't, for example, say that they must be single, unless you can prove that that is a requirement of the job − that is unlikely apart from rare cases.

This means that when drawing up your person profile you must concentrate only on those aspects that are directly relevant to the individual's ability to carry out the job.

There are two factors to focus on, essential requirements for the job and those things that are desirable but you could either manage without or train in. Then you could split down your essential and desirable elements into main headings. I list some here as examples, but the list is not exhaustive.

Experience:
Do they need any previous experience? What in? How much experience? Be realistic here. Don't make extensive experience a requirement for the job unless it's really necessary. If you recruit someone with too much experience who could do the job standing on their head, they are unlikely to stay for long. Only ask for experience that is really needed.

Education and qualifications:
Where a person went to school is not important. What is important is whether or not they have the level of educational qualifications that they need to do the job. Don't ask for highly qualified people for a job that doesn't require high levels of qualification. Although it may be a way of short listing, if the person is over-qualified they won't stay for long.

Is there any other training or qualifications that they might usefully have, for example, a professional qualification?

Special skills:
Does the job require specific skills that are only found in a few people, for example, computer programming or the ability to use spreadsheets or operate a particular type of machinery?

Personality: This is a dangerous one, because personality is such a subjective thing. However, you could specify, for example, the ability to work in a team environment, the ability to deal with demanding clients, etc.

Physical: Standard of health and fitness. Anything to do with physical ability to do the job (however, please remember that if you can adapt the job so that a person with disabilities could do it then you cannot discriminate against them).

There may be other headings which you want to use. You may also wish to rate your person profile by order of importance. For example, someone might get 10 points for being able to use a spreadsheet and only five for their experience of Powerpoint. A point scoring system is a very objective way of making that crucial appointment decision.

Having done all this preparation you are much more likely to choose the right candidate. You are now ready to advertise the job.

Advertising

When preparing the advertisement or briefing the agency remember to avoid your prejudices or bias. I do not believe that a person's age is relevant when recruiting them for a job. So I never ask for it, either in the advertisement, the agency brief or the interview. It's too easy to assume that young people are impulsive or older people are narrow-minded and resistant to change. My experience is that people who are enthusiastic by nature tend to stay that way, albeit maybe modified somewhat, and that cynical people are cynical whatever their age.

My advice is not to bother specifying an age range. That way, you don't miss out on potential good candidates.

When people do apply, make sure you send them enough information about the job and the person that you are looking for so that they have the opportunity thoroughly to prepare for the job.

Making the appointment

Prepare a list of the questions that you are going to ask. Here are some simple rules which will help you.

- Don't ask questions about things that quite clearly appear on their CV unless you want to delve deeper.
- Make most of the questions focus on the job spec and person profile.
- Ask for examples.
- Don't ask hypothetical questions – you'll get hypothetical answers! Ask questions that help a person to tell you about a time when they had to do something. For example, don't say, 'What would you do if you were faced with an angry customer?'. Say, 'Tell me about a time when you had to deal with someone who was angry. What was the situation and how did you handle it?'. Then you get the real person answering and it will be harder for them to try and structure their answer to reflect what they imagine you might want to hear.
- Don't have too many questions. Fewer questions requiring more in-depth answers are more effective.
- Make sure that so far as reasonably practical you ask each candidate the same kinds of questions.

I would advise against panel interviews or interviews which put people under too much pressure. When I interview someone I want to give them the chance to do well. I want to see them perform at their best. However, I normally do have at least one other person with me during an interview, who will often jointly conduct it. This is so that any of my assumptions or unconscious prejudices can be discussed with my colleague.

When appropriate I will also introduce potential candidates to the team with whom they will be working so that they can spend some time chatting with them and I can also hear the team's views.

Allow yourself plenty of time to conduct the interview. If you rush it you may miss something important.

Be clear about the objectives of the interview. There are two.

1 To find out whether the candidate is the right person for the job.

2   To find out whether the organization and job is right for the candidate.

Make sure you take plenty of notes and offer the candidate the opportunity to do the same. You will find it hard to remember what each person said when you have seen lots of people.

Checklist of interviewing skills

- Be prepared!
- Put the candidate at their ease.
- Ask open questions.
- Explain the structure of the interview.
- Introduce everyone in the room.
- Listen carefully to what they are saying.
- Don't make assumptions.
- Ask questions that require detailed answers.
- Thank them at the end.
- Tell them what will be happening next and when you will contact them.
- Write up the interview notes immediately the interview has closed.

Finally, don't leave people waiting for an answer longer than is absolutely necessary. As soon as you have made a decision let them know. It isn't always possible to give every candidate feedback on how they did, but try to avoid bland letters saying 'over-qualified' or 'not enough experience'. Remember how much you hated those kinds of rejections. If people ask for feedback, I think you should give it to them. And you definitely should give face-to-face feedback to internal candidates who didn't get the job.

Induction

A brief word about induction to round off this chapter on recruitment and selection. Poorly conducted induction can often mean the difference between someone staying in a job and leaving it quickly. I don't mean formal company inductions either. I mean you as the manager inducting your new team member into the job and into the team.

Too many managers leave the job of induction to the personnel or human resources department. Certainly there are functions that can be performed by formal induction training. However, as I'm sure you've all experienced, much of what is learned on full day induction programmes is forgotten very quickly, especially if they are conducted in the early days of the individual's appointment to the job.

Most new starters want to get involved in the job as quickly as possible. They really don't want to listen to lots of people giving them information. They want to get on with it. So here is a simple checklist of things you can do to ensure that an individual is inducted as quickly and as effectively as possible.

Before they start the job

- Send them reading material about the organization, especially things like the staff handbook and the health and safety policies. People are normally very enthusiastic before they start a new job and are much more likely to read them then than after they begin work.
- Send them all the paperwork they will need to complete.
- Try and arrange for them to meet members of the team before their first day in the job. Can they come in for lunch one day? Can you meet for a drink after work? Is there a leaving do they can come to?
- Send them a copy of their training and induction plan.
- Send them a copy of the job description if they haven't got one.
- Are there any minutes of team meetings or other internal communications such as newsletters that they can scan that will give them some idea of what the organization is like?
- A nice touch is to drop them a card or letter saying how much you and the team are looking forward to having them work with you.
- Confirm the date and time of starting. (I suggest you ask them to start a little later on the first day so that you have time to get ready for them.)

● Make sure that they are fully aware of what to do when they arrive, who to ask for, what to wear and what to bring with them.

On the first day

● Ensure the area where they are going to be sitting is ready for them.
● Introduce them to the members of the team.
● Give them a little room map with people's desk positions and names on them. That way, if they forget someone's name they only need to look at their map.
● Show them the essentials like toilets, canteen facilities if you have them, stationery cupboards and photocopy rooms, etc.
● Check that they are aware of the fire procedure.
● Take them to lunch or arrange that the team take them.
● Show them how to answer the telephones and what to say. The chances are if everyone in the team is busy and the phone is ringing they'll want to be able to pick it up.
● Make sure that they do at least one piece of work that is in their job, even if it's only minor.

During the first week

● They should by now be introduced to the basics of the job.
● Check that they have read and understood key documents like the health and safety policy and the staff handbook.
● Make sure all the necessary paperwork has been completed.
● Introduce them to other key departments with whom they are likely to be involved.
● Have a 1-1 with them to monitor their progress.
● Check that their training plan is organized.

During the first month

● They should have at least weekly 1-1s with you during the first month so that you can check on progress. After that you can reduce to fortnightly or monthly, whichever is most appropriate.

● Introduce them to other parts of the organization which they may not yet have encountered.
● Make sure they have received any necessary formal training or induction from others.
● They should by now be fully aware of the organization's procedures and policies such as grievance and discipline.
● They should also have had targets set for them and understand how the organization's performance review system operates.

A good induction will go a long way towards ensuring that not only did you recruit the right person but you are also able to keep them.

Summary and key actions

● Be sure that the job specification accurately reflects the job.
● Design your person specification so that it is realistic – don't design it so that the person you recruit is over-qualified for the job.
● During the interview, don't ask hypothetical questions, ask for specific examples.
● When inducting, try to do as much as you can before the person starts the job.
● Let them do a piece of work on the first day.

Jargon glossary

Some of the terms listed have many different explanations. This glossary uses the definition which applies specifically to the workplace.

Accrual	An estimate made of money spent in a month where the invoice has not yet been received
ACL – Action-centred Leadership	A leadership approach that focuses on the actions and skills a leader needs
Action minutes	Minutes at a meeting that record only the actions agreed, who is going to take them and the deadlines
Assertiveness	A form of interpersonal communication that allows a win/win result
Bottom line	Term used to describe the profit line on organizational accounts
Business Process Re-engineering	Re-design of business processes such as production, logistics, customer service, etc.

Business plan	The written statement of an organization's priorities for a future period and how they aim to achieve it
Business indicators	Usually organization specific, these are the figures that show how well a business is doing and will sometimes be based on sales made
Cash flow	The cash you have received and cash you have paid out over a given period
Consultations	Systematic method of asking employees their view on matters affecting them and the organization
Debtor days	A calculation of the number of days you are not paid for your products/services
Delegation	Giving someone responsibility for carrying out a task that could be done by you
Depreciation	The cost of something spread over a period of time, usually its useful life
Diversity	The term used to describe the different kinds of people in the workplace
EFQM – European Foundation for Quality Management	The awarding body for the Business Excellence Model which is a model to describe the key elements that an organization needs to get right in order to run a quality organization
EO – Equal opportunities	A term now used to describe legislation, but essentially the right of people not to be discriminated against on the basis of gender or race in the workplace
Ethics	The way an organization conducts itself in delivering its products and services
Fixed asset	Assets which remain in the organization over a long period of time and are not traded

Forecast	An estimate of income and expenditure against budget for a future period
Gross profit	Profit before tax and fixed costs
Head count	The number of people employed in an organization at a given time
Job summary (description)	A statement of the key tasks and responsibilities in a job
Learning styles	A system of identifying how people learn, designed by Peter Honey and Alan Mumford
Liabilities	The amount of money owed to others
Mission statement	A short sentence to describe the aim of the organization
Negotiations	The dialogue between people where they discuss terms of a business relationship
Net profit	Profit after tax (or distributable profit)
Network	The group of people with whom you have some kind of relationship
Objectives	A measurable statement of something you are trying to achieve
Operating profit	Gross profit less operating expenses
Performance appraisal	The interview, usually annually, where an individual's performance is assessed
Person profile	Statement of the skills, qualifications and personal attributes required in an individual to fulfil a specific role
Proactive	Planned action
Reactive	Action in response to circumstances
Revenue	Amount of sales
Risk assessment	Carrying out of an audit to assess threats to health, safety, etc., and what can be done to avoid them

Shareholders	People who own shares in a company
SMP – Statutory Maternity Pay	Pay that is given to women in the UK who take maternity leave, normally paid out by the organization and recovered from the government
SSP – Statutory Sick Pay	Pay that is given to people in the UK who are off sick, normally paid by the organization
Staff turnover	The number of people who leave an organization over a given period of time, normally expressed as a percentage
Strategy	The long term plan for achieving objectives
Team briefing	A method of passing information about an organization to team members
TQM – Total Quality Management	A method of designing and running systems in an organization to ensure that goods and services are of high quality
Trading or operating profit	Profit before taxes and interest, paid or received
Turnover	The value of sales achieved, not including fixed assets
Variable asset	Assets that are used quickly in the running of the organization
Variance	The difference between what was planned and what was achieved, normally against budget
Vision statement	An expression of how the organization sees itself in the future
Working capital	The money used up in stocks, debtors and cash minus current liabilities

Do's and Don'ts – a quick guide

Do	Don't
Get some management and leadership training	Try to do the job without training
Take the time to get to know the team	Base your opinion of them on what other people have said
Make sure you have a thorough induction plan	Be afraid to ask questions
Focus on being a leader, not just a manager	Get bogged down in rules, regulations and policies
Admit mistakes	Blame others when they make them
Be enthusiastic	Moan about the organization or your boss to the team
Put across the management line as if it were your own	Act as if you are still a member of the team and not management
Act on your values	Say one thing and mean or do another
Listen to understand	Listen to catch out
Take time to get to know other departments	Be too busy to build relationships with other departments

Do	Don't
Ask people what makes them feel satisfied at work and what you can do to help	Blame lack of motivation on the individual
Communicate regularly	Assume that people will know or understand information without checking that they do
Hold regular 1-1s	Forget to spend time talking to individuals within your team
Look out for signs of stress in your team	Ignore potential problems because you are too busy
Know what your health and safety responsibilities are	Ignore potential hazards
Make sure people have clear job summaries	Assume that standards are known and understood if they are not written down
Get to know how the organization runs its accounts	Tie up money in unnecessary stock
Give new employees an induction plan	Appoint people who are over-qualified for the job

References

Appraisal and Appraisal Interviewing, Ian Lawson, The Industrial Society, 1989

Empower Yourself, Eve Warren and Caroline Gielnick, The Industrial Society, 1995

Finance and Budgeting for Line Managers, Anthony Greenall, The Industrial Society, 1996

Introduction to Psychology, Volume 1, The Open University Press, 1996

Leadership and the New Science, Margaret Wheatley, Berrett-Koehler, 1994

Liberating Leadership – A Manager's Guide to the New Leadership, David Turner, The Industrial Society, 1998

Management Skills – A Practical Handbook, The Industrial Society, 1993

Managing Best Practice (Maximising Attendance), The Industrial Society, February 1997

Managing for High Performance, Roger Moores, The Industrial Society, 1994

Pocket Manager, Tim Hindle, The Economist Books, 1997

Risk Assessment, Pat McGuinness, The Industrial Society, 1995

Sensitive Issues in the Workplace, Sue Morris, The Industrial Society, 1993

The Human Zoo, Desmond Morris, Vintage, 1994

The Whole Brain Business Book, Ned Herrmann, McGraw Hill, 1996

The Work Environment – The Law of Health, Safety and Welfare, Patricia Leighton, Nicholas Brealey Publishing in association with The Industrial Society, 1997

Time and Workload Management, Debra Allcock, The Industrial Society, 1995